SUCCESSFUL GARDENING

CREATIVE
GARDEN DESIGN

Published by The Reader's Digest Association Limited.

First Edition Copyright © 1993
The Reader's Digest Association Limited,
Berkeley Square House, Berkeley Square, London W1X 6AB

Copyright © 1993
The Reader's Digest Association Far East Limited
Philippines Copyright 1993
The Reader's Digest Association Far East Limited

Consultant editor: Lizzie Boyd

Typeset by SX Composing Limited in Century Schoolbook

PRINTED IN SPAIN

ISBN 0 276 42090 X

Opposite: Good garden design marries house with garden.
The white-washed walls of a thatched cottage are tailor-made
for climbing wisteria, ivies, clematis and roses.

Overleaf: A tiny town garden becomes a secret enclosure
of greenery ornamented with statuary, pots of lilies and
ancient flagstones.

Pages 6-7: A suburban garden has lost its squared-up shape
through a design of curved lines and raised planting
and scree beds.

PUBLISHED BY THE READER'S DIGEST ASSOCIATION LIMITED
LONDON NEW YORK MONTREAL SYDNEY CAPE TOWN

Originally published in partwork form
by Eaglemoss Publications Limited

SUCCESSFUL GARDENING

CREATIVE
GARDEN DESIGN

Creative garden design

Every garden is an expression of the owners' creativity and, within the limitations of its size, their imagination can be given free rein. There are no hard and fast rules for 'correct' design, and no two gardens will ever be alike.

Often the difference between the ordinary and the outstanding garden lies in a relatively minor design detail – a focal point that draws the eye, gentle reflections in a peaceful pool, a carefully positioned path, or simply a corner of peace and tranquillity separated from the rest of the garden and complemented with suitable plants.

Creative gardeners can translate the ideas and suggestions described in this book to their own particular situation to design their own ideal gardens.

CONTENTS

Basic design

Small gardens

Large gardens

Design for a purpose

Theme gardens

Curved lines The rectangular shape of a suburban garden is softened by a lawn designed on gently curving lines.

Garden planning

Few gardens meet with their owners' complete approval, for we all have different ideas about what constitutes a perfect garden. Absolute perfection is not the goal, however, since gardening is a long-term, constantly developing interest where one's needs and aims change. The goal is a garden which suits and pleases the owner.

Before discarding an existing layout, it is a good idea to live with a garden for at least a year, to watch it during the seasons and analyse its positive and negative sides. In this way you will discover which plants are worthy of retention and which should be replaced, and find the sunniest and most sheltered spot for a patio or kitchen garden. Some aspects of the existing plan can often be turned to advantage without a great deal of work or expense – a vista can be screened off or opened out, and minor improvements to the boundaries can create illusions of space.

Next, draw a scale plan which shows both garden features and existing plants. Before digging even a single shovel of soil or emptying the smallest border, plot in all your ideas. It is sensible to establish a basic framework from the beginning, letting the individual features develop over several years. The best laid plans should be adaptable to minor improvements and alterations as the garden matures and family needs change.

Rural idyll Flowers in pastel shades perfectly reflect the gentle contours of a cottage garden.

CREATING AN IDEAL GARDEN

The style and format of any garden must be tailored to meet the family's needs and must be compatible with the architecture of the house.

There are so many different types of garden, all of them beautiful in their own way, that it is easy to be overwhelmed by choice. As well as the different styles – formal or informal, traditional cottage garden or modern, labour-saving layout – there are hundreds of plants and dozens of garden ornaments available from garden centres and larger DIY stores. It isn't, however, simply a matter of choosing attractive plants or bits of outdoor furniture. How the various plants and features are arranged can make the difference between a successful garden – one that is a pleasure to look at, to relax in and to maintain – and an indifferent or unsatisfactory one.

Time spent on working out a good design can involve less money and effort in the long run,

and more time to enjoy the garden.

This attention to detail in the planning stages will help the garden to suit its setting. Such planning will also ensure that all areas of the garden are accessible both visually to onlookers, and physically to the tendings of the gardener.

Setting and accessibility apart, the gardener is free to choose any style and incorporate any of the many different features that exist – patios, rock gardens, pools, rose arbours, vegetable plots – but must take care that the overall impression the garden gives is one of pleasing harmony.

A garden is a living thing and as such it is constantly developing. So whether it needs a complete overhaul, a change of design or just simple upkeep, there is plenty to keep the keen gardener busy.

▲ **Instant gardening** Containers of all kinds, filled with bright bedding plants, provide useful colour and help to brighten up a garden as yet in its formative stages.

▼ **Old-world charm** Well-tried favourites – old shrub roses, fast-growing mock orange, lavender, lady's mantle and white campanulas – lend an air of maturity to a garden scene.

▶ **Kitchen garden** A vegetable plot is a must for many gardeners. It should be open to sun and air, but can easily be placed near the boundaries and screened from the main garden with rows of flowers grown especially for cutting.

◀ **Garden pool** Thanks to modern technology, pre-shaped pools can be installed in a few hours and enhanced with a rock garden built from simulated stone boulders. Take time, though, to consider aspect and feasibility in the overall garden picture.

▼ **Children's play area** In the outdoor living room, children need a place of their own. Site sand-pits for toddlers close to the house — later a brick sand-pit can be converted into a raised planting bed or a small pool.

◄ **Outdoor living space** A patio should be spacious enough to allow for summer meals and entertaining. Use non-slip materials in keeping with the house and ensure uncluttered access.

▼ **Vertical emphasis** A rampant *Clematis montana* tumbles over fence and house wall, its early-summer pink flowers echoing the warm terracotta colour of the patio. Centrepiece in the garden, the beauty of the stone is enhanced with an urn of restrained elegance planted with trailing helichrysum and dainty-leaved white-flowered marguerites.

Specimen planting Carefully chosen specimen trees create focal points and visual emphasis.

ANALYSIS OF A GARDEN

**As the new owner of a garden, take time to
assess its character and weigh up its strong and weak
points before making important changes.**

If you know your garden's potential, you can make the most of it, and if you recognize its problems, you can start to correct them. Resist the temptation to begin on major improvements and planting schemes until you have sorted out your priorities.

If you've just moved house, it's a good idea to live with the garden as it is for a year. Cheap and cheerful bulbs and annuals can fill gaps, while you wait to see what comes up and slowly consider long-term plans. Some professional garden designers find it useful to take reference photographs to help them see (and remember) a garden as it really is. You can build a visual reference file by taking photographs from one position, such as the centre of the lawn, and other shots from the main rooms that overlook the garden. Take photographs in winter as well as in summer.

Existing plants

Established trees and shrubs give a garden character, a feeling of permanence and privacy. Those in the wrong place can sometimes be moved while dormant and others that seem too big, overgrown or misshapen can often be improved by drastic pruning.

Think twice about removing mature trees — as well as being beautiful, some are protected by law. Check with the council that

no preservation order applies; it is also advisable to employ a professional tree surgeon. Remember that if you change your mind afterwards it will take years to grow a tree to replace it.

Vistas and eye-sores

A pleasant view from the garden, whether of a distant or nearby scene, is worth 'framing' with upright trees or shrubs on either side. A permanent garden seat could face the view, or a path be redirected towards it.

Eye-sores within the garden — such as a garage, shed or compost heap — can be camouflaged with climbers or dense-growing shrubs. Eye-sores outside the garden are

▲ **Visual evidence** For a panoramic record of the garden, take several photographs from the same position, moving the camera around so that it takes in the whole expanse.

more difficult, and may require trellising or woven panels on top of existing walls, or tall trees.

Evergreen trees and shrubs give total camouflage, but may also block out too much light. Deciduous plants are a good compromise: they offer reasonable screening, but let in light in winter when light levels are low.

Soil

The type of soil in the garden — whether heavy, sticky clay,

Focal points Emphasize an attractive distant view by framing it with trees, an arch or pergola. Or site a garden seat or path so that the eye is guided towards the view.

Screening eye-sores A hedge or fence can conceal necessary but unattractive objects. This frees the rest of the garden for an attractive layout and ornamental features.

▶ **Distant vista** Massive planting schemes can be adapted in scale to suit smaller gardens. This geometric design is based on a straight path of granite setts leading to a circular platform with a huge urn as a centrepiece against a backdrop of blue-flowered ceanothus. The surrounding formal parterre beds, edged with low clipped box, serve to reinforce the view of the urn from a distance.

▼ **Enclosed vista** A gravel covered drive enclosed by large mature trees focuses on a single impressive focal point — a large olive jar containing an arching phoenix palm, with a footing of bright nasturtiums. Even on a dull day, the pale-coloured gravel appears as a pool of light.

light, free-draining sandy or chalky soil, rich loam, or a mixture of these types – doesn't really affect the layout of the garden. However, certain plants require certain soils – azaleas and rhododendrons, for example, thrive only on free-draining, acid soil – so it is wise to match plants to soil type from the outset.

Most plants, notably perennials and annuals, grow in a wide range of soils, and while you cannot change a soil type, its structure and texture can be improved.

Sun and shade

The pattern of sun and shade in a garden varies according to the time of day and the time of year. Certain spots may get the morning sun; others, the afternoon or evening sun, and still others, no sun at all. Once again, a few photographs taken at different times of day and year will reveal the changing patterns of light and shade. Some plants are equally happy in sun or light shade; others are more choosy.

There's nothing you can do to alter shade from buildings, walls and north-facing slopes, but trees can often be pruned to allow in more sunlight. Shady spots are often dry, because whatever blocks out light also prevents rain from getting in.

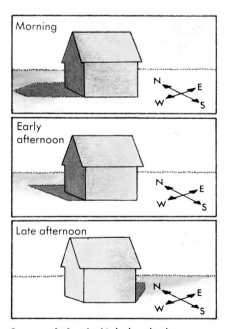

Sun and shade Light levels change according to the time of day. In the morning, summer sun in the east shades the west and north side of a house. As the sun gradually moves westwards, the north and east sides start to go into shadow.

Aspect

A garden positioned on a south-facing slope warms up earlier in spring than a similar garden on level ground. During the cold winter months, a north-facing slope is hardly touched at all by the sun's low rays.

Aspect obviously affects where you put particular plants. Sun-loving plants will never succeed in a very shady site.

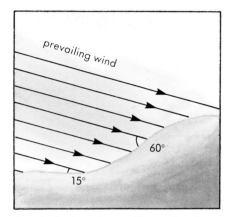

South-facing slopes These absorb more of the sun's heat than level ground, with higher temperatures and more shelter on the leeward side.

Local weather conditions

How cold it gets in winter, how hot in summer, and the dates of the first and last frosts, vary from one part of the country to another. (If you are new to an area, ask the neighbours.) Conditions may vary each year and are affected by the lie of the land – a valley in summer is warmer than a nearby hill, but in winter the reverse is true. Rainfall also varies, but watering can make up the difference.

Some plants are hardier than others, so bear in mind the local climate when choosing permanent plants and timing summer bedding and vegetable sowing.

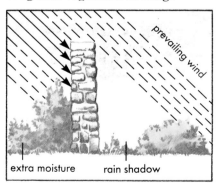

Walls, hedges and fences These create dry areas on the leeward side of the prevailing wind – any plants sited here will need extra watering.

Exposure

Plants do not like wind, which can be drying, chilling and often both. Strong wind can also break off branches and even loosen plants' foothold in the soil – which will eventually kill them.

Walls provide shelter but, according to where they are sited, can also create unwanted shade and wind turbulence. Partial screening – in the form of hedges, fences or trellising – is often a better choice. The wind is then filtered through the fence or hedge and its force reduced without buffeting plants sited nearby.

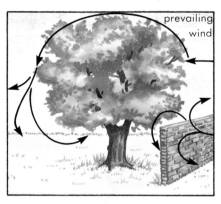

Wind barriers Solid walls, buildings and dense trees block the wind, causing turbulence on the leeward side.

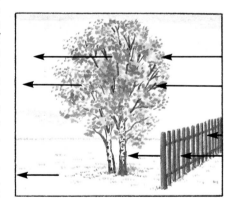

Wind filters Fences and light trees allow wind to pass through, reducing its intensity without causing turbulence.

Man-made features

Some garden buildings, such as brick garages, are there to stay, and any new garden designs have to be worked round them. Smaller features, such as sheds, bird baths, and even paths and gates, can be repositioned, replaced or removed to improve the look and organization of the garden.

If a hard-surfaced path is in the wrong place, worn-out lawn nearby often shows where it would be better positioned.

Choosing garden features

There is no one recipe for creating the perfect garden, although there are useful guidelines for choosing and combining the different features found in most people's gardens. It is partly a matter of striking a balance between too many features, which can make a garden seem restless, and too few, which make a garden boring. It is also a matter of making the garden and house work comfortably together. Most importantly, the finished garden should reflect your own personal taste and style.

In an analysis of your garden, you should take into consideration the unalterable factors of fixed boundaries, aspect, soil type and local climate. These are the foundations upon which you must create a garden; try to regard obstacles as challenges to be overcome rather than as insoluble problems.

Making a start

The list that follows provides an at-a-glance guide to the main features that go into garden-making. Don't try to incorporate them all, and live for a while with a major reconstruction before moving on to the next project. Start by reading through the list, and try to relate the features to your garden – as it is and as you want it to be.

Making your own list of all the features will help you, if you're not sure where or how to start. Note down which features your garden already has that:
☐ You want to retain
☐ You want to improve
☐ You want to add
☐ You want to remove
Then pause for thought and consider if you are trying to cram in too much. Next, try to decide which features on your list are essential, which are desirable and which you could do without.

This is also helpful if you can't create your ideal garden in one go, and have to proceed in stages.

SCREENS AND DIVIDERS

These can form the boundary to a garden, or divide it into a series of different 'rooms'. They can be high or low and stretch right across the garden or only a part of it.

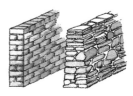

Walls

Brick or stone walls are durable, attractive and create a sense of privacy. They also create sun traps – warm, sheltered areas ideal for tender plants or for sitting out.

New walls are very expensive to build and can look raw to start with. Perforated concrete walling is an attractive and economical alternative. Aim to choose a material that suits the style of your house.

Fences

Fences are cheaper than walls, and need less skill in putting up. They offer instant enclosure and come in a wide range of materials, from solid or woven wood panels, to open wire mesh.

Most fences need regular maintenance, or replacing every so often. Climbing plants can hide plain fences, but may make maintenance difficult.

Hedges

Established hedges are attractive and make a restful background to other plants.

Some hedging plants are slow growing; those that are quick often outgrow available space. Most need regular pruning. Hedges take up more space than walls, and take nutrients and water from the soil.

Paths

Paths should be firm, easy to walk on, generously wide, and free draining, and the material should complement the house and other hard surfaces, such as a nearby patio or steps.

Path layouts should relate to house and garage doors and garden gates. Paths that wander aimlessly rarely get used.

Level changes

Slopes, retaining walls and raised beds or even sunken patios make a garden interesting and provide homes for such 'specialist' plants as alpines.

Steps should be firm, dry and evenly spaced, and complement nearby paving.

MAIN PLANT FEATURES

These are the 'soft furnishings' of your garden, that make it attractive all through the year.

Grass

Lawns are lovely to walk on and look at. Those grown from seed are inexpensive; turfing is more expensive but 'instant'. In larger gardens, rough lawn can be attractive, reducing maintenance and providing a home for spring-flowering bulbs and native wild flowers.

Lawns do badly in dense shade or much trampled small areas. Formal lawns need regular mowing and trimming through spring, summer and autumn.

Flowers

Herbaceous perennials, biennials, annuals and bulbs are all types of plants which can provide quick colour, for both new and established gardens.

You can afford to be adventurous with these plants because most can be rearranged in the garden to give a completely different look, if you aren't satisfied with your first scheme.

Shrubs

Shrubs add a feeling of depth and space to a garden, making a flat rectangle of ground seem more interesting or larger than it really is. They also add height and texture to a mixed border, and serve as a perfect foil for annuals and perennials.

Shrub and mixed borders generally work best when 90cm-1.8m (3-6ft) wide. Narrower, and the plants tend to run out of growing room; wider, and the border is difficult to cultivate.

Trees

Trees, more than any other feature, make a garden look established, and give it a three-dimensional quality.

Many decorative trees available these days grow no taller at maturity (about 20 years) than 7-8m (23-26ft) if space is limited.

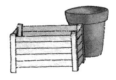

Containers

Plant containers are perfect for adding spots of colour to a garden. They come in a wide range of sizes, materials, shapes and styles.

The larger a container is, the more effective, and the less often it needs watering. A large pot is also less likely to be knocked over. For outdoor use, choose fired frost-proof containers.

SPECIALIST PLANTING

Even the smallest garden can have a mini-collection of 'specialist' plants.

Rose gardens

Everybody loves roses, and many gardeners devote entire beds to the hybrid teas and floribundas, which can flower from early summer to late autumn. Most roses prefer sun and rich, slightly heavy, well-drained soil, but some varieties will flower reasonably well in light shade.

Old roses have better looking leaves and shape – and more interesting hips – than modern varieties. Think about how a rose bed will look while it is in bloom; consider low underplanting and evergreen edging for the dreary winter months.

Rock gardens

Rock gardens provide the perfect setting for attractive alpine plants, as well as dwarf conifers.

Real rocks are expensive and heavy, but most garden centres

stock lightweight imitation rocks which are far cheaper. Rockeries look best on slopes: they rarely look natural in flat gardens. Growing alpine plants in raised beds or sink gardens are popular alternatives.

Heather beds

With their evergreen foliage and flowers which range from white through pink and lavender to deepest purple, heathers can brighten a garden all year round.

Newly planted heather beds need regular weeding until the plants mat together. For added interest, include a few dwarf conifers or rhododendrons.

Vegetables

Growing your own vegetables saves money as well as providing tasty, fresh produce.

You don't need a separate area for growing vegetables. Many – runner beans and loose-leaf lettuce, for example – are decorative enough to be grown in among flowers and shrubs in mixed borders, or in pots or grow bags.

Fruit

Fruit trees can be as ornamental as they are practical, providing flowers, autumn leaf colour and winter interest as well as crops.

For small gardens, fruit trees on dwarfing rootstocks are best. Trees trained as espaliers, fans or cordons can be grown flat against a wall or stout rustic fence. Most fruit trees need a suitable cultivar nearby for cross pollination; check with a garden centre before buying.

Herbs

Herbs can be grown successfully in mixed borders, containers or window-boxes, as well as in 'traditional' herb gardens.

When picking herbs for the kitchen, pick little and often. Completely stripping a plant of its leaves kills it.

LEISURE FEATURES

These are as important as plants if you and your family want to relax in the garden.

Patios and paved areas

Ideally, a patio should be sheltered and sunny for a good bit of the day, and have an attractive

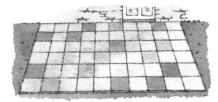

view or a cosy, self-contained feel. All paved areas should be firm, level and free draining, and the paving should match nearby hard surfaces.

The closer a patio is to a house, the better. Make sure it's large enough for a table and chairs. Plants in tubs and large flowerpots are ideal for patios.

Furniture

Well chosen and well-positioned furniture can transform a garden into a pleasant room for outdoor living. Fixed garden furniture should be heavy, durable and weather-proof. Movable garden furniture should be stable but lightweight enough to be carried easily.

Too much furniture permanently on display in a garden makes it look like a garden centre. It is better to have a few, good quality, comfortable pieces. Note that movable garden furniture requires winter storage space.

Barbecues

Barbecues are becoming increasingly popular for family eating as well as entertaining. Built-in brick barbecues are expensive, but worthwhile if used often. Portable barbecues are more flexible, and can be stored during the winter.

For safety, site the barbecue on level ground away from paths and overhanging trees – especially holly and conifers.

Children's play areas

Young children need somewhere sheltered, sunny and dry to play, within sight of the house. Older children appreciate privacy, and enjoy a climbing frame or swing hidden behind a screen.

Major pieces of play equipment must be well anchored in the ground and, ideally, have rubber-ized safety matting underneath.

DECORATIVE FEATURES

These are the finishing touches that provide focal points and help to express a garden's personality.

Garden pools

With its water plants, fish and reflections, an ornamental pool makes an instant focal point. Most are now made of rigid glass fibre, or flexible polythene, PVC

or rubber sheeting, and come in many colours, shapes and sizes. Generally, simple shapes look more natural than complicated ones.

A sunny, open, level site away from overhanging trees is ideal. Ornamental pools need cleaning out from time to time. Unsupervised small children and pools can be a dangerous combination.

Arches and pergolas

These add instant height to a garden, and can emphasize an

entrance or view. They can be iron, brick, aluminium or wood, or a combination of materials, and are ideal for climbing plants.

Arches and pergolas look most effective linking other features (such as a hedge) rather than standing by themselves.

Statues and ornaments

A statue, birdbath or sundial can add that special something to a garden.

Try not to get carried away and buy too many ornaments as the effect can be very 'spotty'. Making a focal point of a sundial, say, or putting a statue in an enclosed corner so that the viewer comes on

it as a surprise, are the most effective ideas.

BUILDINGS

The best garden buildings are attractive as well as being suited to their purpose.

Greenhouses/conservatories

These are places for growing tender and out-of-season vegetables and pot plants for the house, or seedlings for the garden. They can also be used to display plants. There is a wide range of

ready-made and purpose-built models, all of which need a sunny sheltered site.

The most common mistake is to buy a greenhouse that is too small. If in doubt, buy bigger.

Sheds and summer houses

These are available ready-made or purpose-built, in a range of materials, sizes and costs.

Unattractive garden buildings can be painted, or covered with climbers.

THE NECESSARIES
These are the 'ugly ducklings' of the garden, essential but not attractive. Screening helps to reduce their impact on the garden scene.
Dustbins need a dry spot easily reached from the house.
Compost heaps are useful for recycling garden and kitchen refuse. Site them near the kitchen garden.
Garages should be near the house but not take prime position.
Clothes-lines need dry access, and a spot where clothes can catch the breeze without snagging.

PLANNING A GARDEN

Every garden contains a number of ornamental and practical features – the trick is arranging them to appear wholly complementary.

Arranging features in your garden is rather like arranging furniture in your living room – there is no right or wrong way, just what is most practical and attractive for you and your family.

Unlike furniture, though, many garden features are almost impossible to shift once in position – paths and ornamental ponds are examples. Or, as with shrubs and trees, they don't really appreciate being moved once they've settled in. It pays to take your time to think about all the options.

Traditional layouts

The traditional approach, illustrated in the sample garden (right), works mainly on straight, symmetrical lines. Herbaceous and shrub borders flank the sides of the garden and a path runs down the centre. Practical areas are reserved for either end of the garden – vegetable patch and greenhouse at the far end; paved seating area and toolshed near the house.

Every feature is treated as a display in its own right, almost like sculptures in a museum. Each element is given equal importance and space to walk round, and the garden becomes a showcase for a collection of features.

While each element can be seen and appreciated on its own, such an approach can give a garden a bitty, restless, unco-ordinated look. And because of the layout, the whole garden can be looked at and absorbed in an instant, with no elements of surprise.

What this garden lacks is a sense of depth – by arranging the features in clusters or groups, you can make the garden seem bigger and more exciting. Making use of different heights, and changes in level, alters the perspective and

enhances the interest. Such devices also allow you to introduce an element of surprise. As you explore the garden – however small – you discover new features that can't be seen immediately.

Suggesting depth

Some gardens have an inbuilt feeling of depth – large country gardens, for example – with major trees as part of the scene, and views to distant fields, villages or hills. But how do you set about creating a feeling of depth in a smaller garden?

Begin by enclosing the garden. You could use a solid boundary, such as a high wall, or a partial shield, perhaps a light fence. Try thinking of your garden as a theatre stage, ready for

▶ **Traditional garden style** A typical layout is based on straight lines within which are displayed, one by one, the various features that make up the average garden. It is functional and uninspiring, but a little creative imagination can transform it.

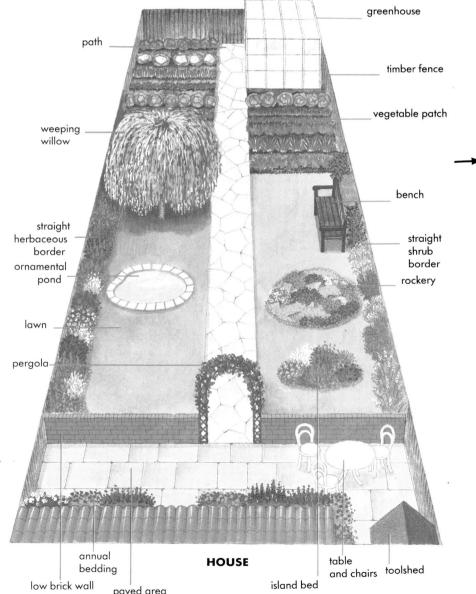

greenhouse

timber fence

vegetable patch

path

bench

weeping willow

straight shrub border

straight herbaceous border

rockery

ornamental pond

lawn

pergola

N

annual bedding

HOUSE

table and chairs

toolshed

low brick wall

paved area

island bed

you to arrange the scenery. To break up the view, use a few large, simple features – some shrubs, heavy pots, a hedge or a trellis, a clump of pampas grass or an arbour. This foreground bit of 'stage scenery' may jut out from the side of the garden, or stretch across the entire width with a pergola in the centre providing a passageway and framing the view beyond.

Small gardens probably only have room for a single interruption – avoid cramming in too many features – while larger, and particularly long ones, can hold several. Each area is then separated and can provide a minisetting for a feature or its own focal point.

GIVING THE GARDEN DEPTH

View from the house
1 Use a piece of paper or card to represent the area of the garden, cut to roughly the actual shape. Imagine your viewpoint to be straight down the garden from the house. The idea is to build gradually on this surface, using a variety of features to create interesting spaces and focal points.

2 Even the largest gardens benefit from some sense of enclosure, and in small gardens it can make all the difference. As well as screening less attractive nearby views and giving privacy, enclosures define the perimeters and provide an empty 'stage setting' on which to arrange and rearrange the scenery.

3 Large, simple features can break up the central space in a garden and give the imagination room to play. Remember that the closer an object is to you, the more it blocks out. Here, an evergreen hedge, ending in a pergola, creates a sense of anticipation and mystery, encouraging you to look round the corner.

4 The addition of a second hedge, and a tree at the far end, leads the eye from one space to the next, by setting up a series of receding areas.

Because the eye has distances to measure, a feeling of depth is created. You can imagine yourself looking through the pergola, and wondering what features might be hidden out of sight.

5 Breaking up a single space into smaller areas often leads to further changes. Here, different surface materials emphasize the separate divisions, and the paving stone path is given a real reason to curve on its journey to the bench at the far end. But all you can see initially is the hedge and a planted container.

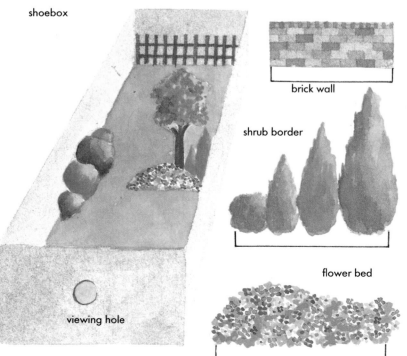

shoebox

viewing hole

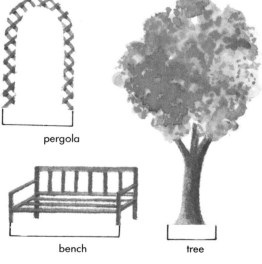

brick wall

shrub border

pergola

bench

tree

flower bed

Use a shoebox to represent the garden, and cut-out cardboard shapes for the chosen features. These need only be simple, with a right-angled fold at the base. Looking through the viewing hole – which corresponds to eye height – try out different permutations.

► **Curves and depth**
Flowing curves create
pockets of mystery in this
garden. From the paved
area, where a small statue
marks the transition into
greenery, the upper part of
the shrubbery is hidden from
view, while at the other end
a trellis with climbers offers a
tantalizing glimpse of a
secluded sitting area.

Curved lines visually
increase the size of the
garden and invite closer
inspection of the mysteries
hidden behind the screen.

▼ **Hidden retreats** A
pergola densely clothed with
fast-growing ivies and
honeysuckle frames the
entrance to a concealed
suntrap. Velvety grass gives
way to mellow stone,
punctuated with weathered
pots of busy Lizzies, and to a
surface covering of gravel.

Varying the height

Most people plan the design of their garden with the tallest plants – trees – at the back, medium-height plants – shrubs – in the middle and bedding plants towards the front. This is one way of giving the garden height. An alternative is to bring some taller plants forward, so that they break up the outline.

Remember, too, that tall elements at the back make a garden look shorter; tall features close to the house make a garden look longer. Consider carefully the choice of trees, their shape, outline, foliage, flowers if any, and their ultimate size. Parkland trees are out of keeping with the average garden.

Varying the height of plants (and other features) has the same effect as adding depth – it gradually leads the eye through the length of the garden. Tall plants act like visual exclamation marks, contrasting with smaller ones.

▼ **Height and space** Varying the height of trees and shrubs, from creeping conifers to slender columnar types, gives an impression of space.

ADDING HEIGHT

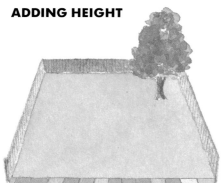

View from the house
1 One good-sized tree is the key to making height work for you in a garden. The tree becomes a focal point, drawing the eye the length of the garden.

2 A shrub about 1.2m (4ft) high at the front or halfway down the garden adds contrast and gives the eye something to measure the tree against – a sort of bouncing-off point.

3 When planning height in your garden, be careful to check the ultimate growth of trees. Ask the nursery the probable height and spread after 15 years – several grow no taller than 7.5m (25ft).

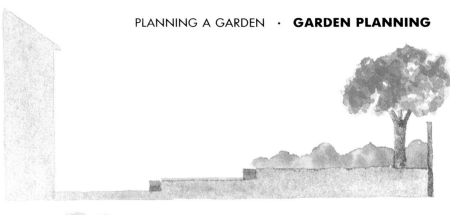

Changing the level

Level changes automatically add appeal to a garden – a cosy secluded feel where the level is low, rising to a sense of space and an open expanse. Some country and suburban gardens retain the natural slope or contours of the land, while gardens of older town houses often have a sunken area outside the back door, with steps up to the rest of the garden.

Rather than considering such built-in level changes a drawback, make a feature of them. Changing the surface texture of each level – paving, then grass, say – defines the divisions and gives a different purpose to each one.

Making level changes in a flat garden needs careful thought. Most levels immediately outside a house can't be tampered with, because of damp proof courses and foundations. You can, though, use earth from one part of the garden to raise another, well away from the house walls, at the same time sinking the part from which you take the earth. Raised planting beds are one possibility, and informally curved planting mounds another.

LEVEL CHANGES

The cross-section (above) and frontal view (left) show how you can give character to a garden by splitting it into three levels. Each level is defined by altering the surface material. In a flat garden, soil from the lowered level can be used to bank up the higher one – alternatively, buy in soil. However, bought-in topsoil can be expensive and may need to be taken through the house, barrow-load by barrow-load. It is important, when building up soil levels next to a boundary wall or fence, to make sure the wall is strong enough to take the additional pressure.

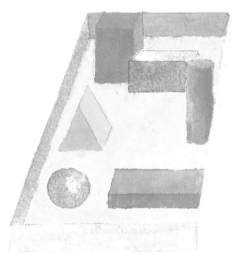

▲ Heights and levels – in the lid of the shoebox, arrange children's building blocks in various patterns, imagining them as differently sized plants. It will help you to work out how to arrange the varying heights of trees, shrubs and bedding plants, and to visualize how the bulk of several close together will look. Because the blocks have simple shapes, and don't look like particular plants, you won't get side-tracked into thinking about the flowers or leaves. An oblong laid flat serves a dual purpose – use it to represent either a flower bed or a raised level. Remember to lower your head so that eye level is just above the rim of the box – the idea is to look through the blocks not down on to them.

▶ Retaining walls are well within the scope of the DIY enthusiast, and increase the range of design possibilities in a garden.

▼ The level change here gives emphasis to the focal point – a circular bench enclosing a fruit tree.

Re-arranging a garden

Compare the garden below with the diagram on page 19 and you will see that much the same features appear in both, and on a site of identical shape and size. In this version, though, the various features have been arranged to make the best use of depth, height and level changes. The end result is a clear expanse of lawn, easy to maintain and restful to the eye, and a series of spaces and features which lead the eye effortlessly from one to another.

The rose-covered pergola frames the view of the garden seen from the house, focusing the eye on a birdbath at the end of the path. It creates an impressive entrance into the main garden and links the raised shrub beds, which

make the patio more sheltered and secluded.

The slightly raised seating area and raised beds transform a flat garden into one on three levels, and the nearby tree and pergola add variation in height. The hedge 'divider' conceals the greenhouse and vegetable patch and prevents the entire garden being seen at once, so helping to give a feeling of depth and size.

A curving border of mixed herbaceous perennials and annuals softens the straight lines of the boundary fence and of the path, which remains unchanged as it is the shortest route down the garden. The combination of rockery and pool makes a year-round focal point and helps to disguise the shape of the long linear garden.

CHECKLIST

The following features make up the traditional layout on page 19 and the reorganized version below.

Lawn
Patio
Path
Toolshed
Flower beds
Herbaceous border
Shrubbery
Greenhouse
Vegetable patch
Pergola
Hedge
Fence
Specimen tree
Ornamental pool
Rockery
Seating
Low wall

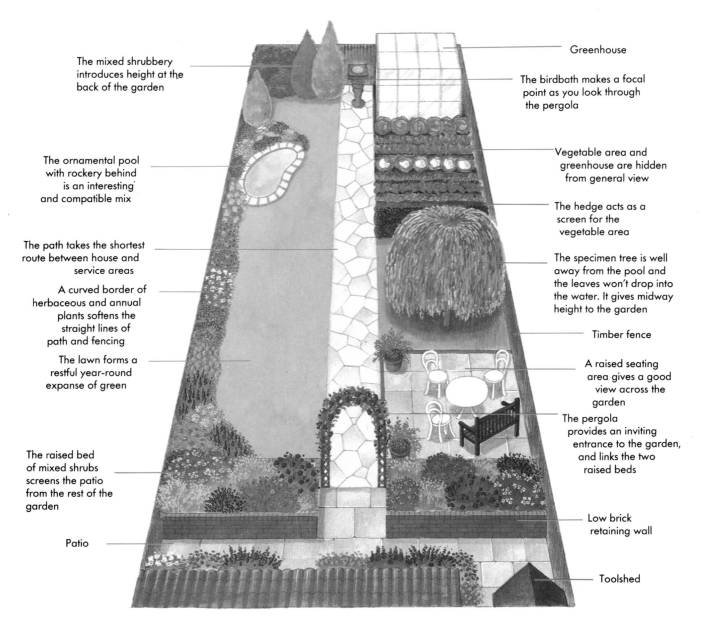

The mixed shrubbery introduces height at the back of the garden

The ornamental pool with rockery behind is an interesting and compatible mix

The path takes the shortest route between house and service areas

A curved border of herbaceous and annual plants softens the straight lines of path and fencing

The lawn forms a restful year-round expanse of green

The raised bed of mixed shrubs screens the patio from the rest of the garden

Patio

Greenhouse

The birdbath makes a focal point as you look through the pergola

Vegetable area and greenhouse are hidden from general view

The hedge acts as a screen for the vegetable area

The specimen tree is well away from the pool and the leaves won't drop into the water. It gives midway height to the garden

Timber fence

A raised seating area gives a good view across the garden

The pergola provides an inviting entrance to the garden, and links the two raised beds

Low brick retaining wall

Toolshed

HOUSE

Initial planning

Most gardens consist of lawn, beds and borders, a patio and such major features as a pool or rock garden. In addition, there are service areas like the compost heap, bonfire site and greenhouse. Only rarely can all these components be incorporated from the outset, but you should allocate them in the initial layout to avoid major alterations later.

Where you are creating a new garden from a bare plot you will probably have a fairly free hand in evolving your personal style. Established gardens can be difficult to transform, and you may be compelled to retain certain features and adapt or remove others before the backbones of the garden begin to emerge.

The first step in garden planning is usually deciding on the patio, which should be in scale with the house and have easy access. Once you have sited the terrace, the rest of the garden framework can be related to it, and the shape of beds and borders will often emerge as a matter of course.

Making a plan

Drawing up a plan will help you to think of the garden as a whole unit, not just a collection of flower beds, paths, lawn and shrubs. It also forces you to think about the long-term look of the garden, as well as instant improvements. With a plan, you can proceed in an orderly way, as and when funds and time allow.

Before deciding on the final design, sketch several possible layouts, retaining existing features that you want to keep or trying new ones, and concealing or removing eye-sores. Trial and error on paper costs virtually nothing. Mistakes can be literally thrown away, so be adventurous.

Make a sketch of the existing garden on plain paper attached to a clipboard.

Sketch the boundaries and general shape in freehand. Looking down on the garden from an upstairs window helps; so does pacing the distances, using your normal stride as a unit of measurement. Moving around while sketching gives a clearer picture of where things are than working solely from, say, the kitchen window.

Draw in the relevant house walls, marking in windows and doors. Indicate trees, including overhanging ones from next door, paths, walls and level changes, patios, sheds and greenhouses, lawns and beds, and ornaments and fixed play equipment.

Mark in any other details, such as the prevailing wind direction, where north is, sunny and shady spots, and good and bad views.

Measuring up

On the sketch, draw dimension lines along the boundaries of the garden. If it is four-sided but not square or rectangular, draw two diagonals to fix the exact angles of the corners. Similarly, if the garden has a complicated layout, divide it into simpler, easily measurable shapes that converge.

Use a long surveyor's tape-measure or, if you don't have one, lengths of string. With a partner to hold one end of the tape and record measurements, measure on the ground each dimension line marked on paper. Work in either metric or imperial units.

Using a corner of the house as a fixed point, you can extend a parallel line down the length of the garden, then plot more positions, such as a nearby path or tree, by taking offset measurements at 90° angles from the main line. To locate more complicated positions, use triangulation.

▼ **Drawing to scale** A rough sketch of an existing garden should incorporate all fixtures and planting areas whether or not you wish to retain them.

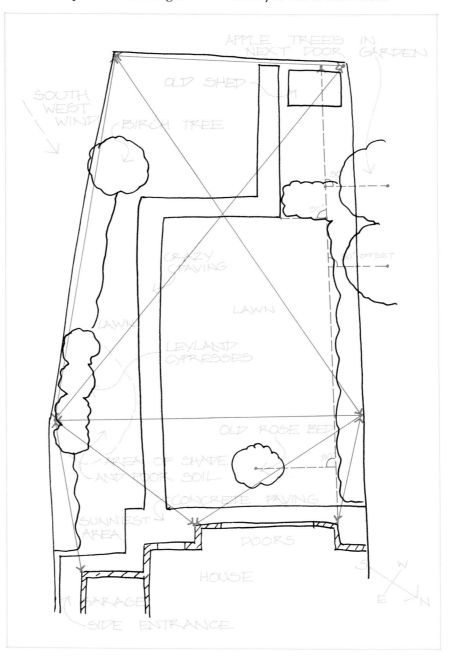

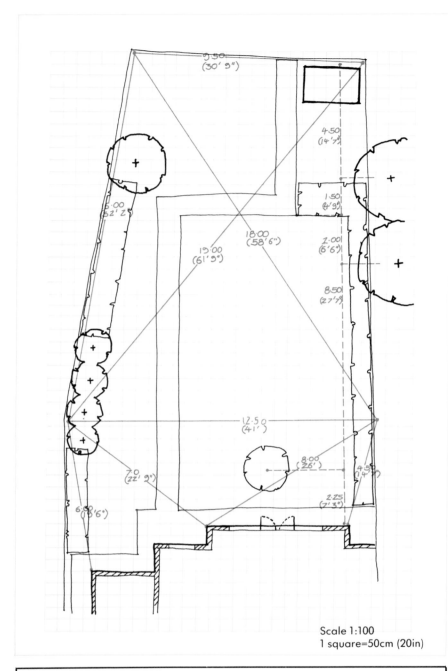

Scale 1:100
1 square=50cm (20in)

◀ **Graph plan** Transfer the rough sketch of the garden to 5mm graph paper to make an accurately scaled plan. Certain areas can be pulled out and the scale enlarged to see them in more detail.

Transferring the sketch

Make the final copy on 5mm graph paper, choosing a scale and paper size that allows the garden to fit on to one sheet. For smaller gardens, 1:50 is best; each 5mm square on paper will equal a 25cm (10in) square on the ground.

Average gardens, say 18 × 12m (60 × 40ft), can be drawn to a scale of 1:100; each 5mm square equals a 50cm (20in) square on the ground. Large gardens may have to be drawn on two sheets of graph paper taped together, or drawn to a smaller scale, with some sections drawn again to 1:50, for working out details.

Check first that the two widest dimensions on the rough sketch will fit on the graph paper at the intended scale, leaving a margin around the actual plan.

In most cases, it is best to start by drawing the house dimensions, then working outwards from the fixed points to the boundaries and various features, either by triangulation or 90° offset readings. Use an H or 2H pencil and a straight edge for a clear, sharp drawing, and a compass for the triangulation method.

Plotting the layout

Tape tracing paper over the scaled plan, then mark on it those features, such as a greenhouse or tree, that you want or have to keep. Next, look at the remaining space in terms of a few simple, large geometric shapes, such as squares and rectangles. Use the basic shape of the garden as a starting point, repeating any attractive curves or angles on a smaller scale.

The smaller the garden, the simpler the layout should be. In time, plants will soften harsh edges and make shapes less obvious. Intricate layouts may look interesting on paper but often look confused on the ground, and are difficult to maintain.

Balance colourful planting areas with visually restful ones, such as a lawn; coloured pencils or felt tips can help you work out the scheme. Think about introducing level changes – a raised planting

Triangulation

To find the *exact* position of a feature which is difficult to locate from 90° offset readings, measure it from any two fixed points.

Here, the rose bush is located by measuring the distance from the house and from the corner of the path. The far cypress is located accurately by measuring it from the rose bush and from the path corner.

On the final drawing, use a compass set to the right measurement according to the scale, to make intersecting arcs which pinpoint the precise spot.

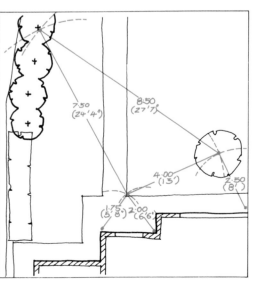

bed or a sunken pool complete with sloping rockery, for instance – if the garden is totally flat.

Work from a checklist of the ornamental and practical features you want to include and list them in order of priority. As you position each one, consider whether it is best in sun or shade, in full view or hidden, near the house or well away, and so on. It is easier to correct and improve a garden layout than to design it from scratch, especially for the first time.

Remember to mark on the plan any manholes and gas, electricity and water pipes, all of which can determine the siting of plants and fixtures. Put the plan aside for a few days, then look at it again with fresh eyes and, if necessary, make alterations at this stage, or a completely new plan.

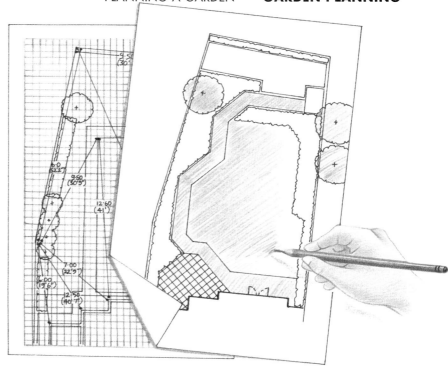

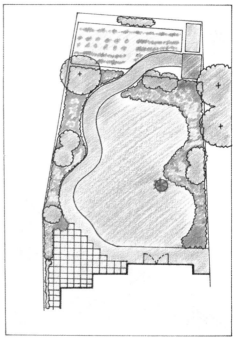

▲ **Planning the design** Having transferred the shape of the garden to graph paper, lay tracing paper over the top and try out different plans to find the best design. First include features that are staying put — such as trees — since these limit and affect the rest of the layout. Then decide how to arrange other features in the most practical and attractive way.

◄ **Perspective** Although it is necessary to design a garden flat, from a bird's-eye view, depth and height changes spring to life only in a three-dimensional plan. For this reason, the layouts on these pages are drawn in perspective, rather than from overhead.

Making a long-term plan

Ideally, you would probably like your garden to have mature lawns and plants, paving and features, all within the first year. Most people, though, work within a small budget, and spread the cost and work of improvements over four or five years.

An 'unfinished' garden can still be attractive, and with a list of priorities and a sensible order of procedure, you will save time, money and effort.

Be realistic about what you can do. Using concrete paving is better than going for years without paths, even if you really want bricks.

Start by removing unwanted features, then work on the framework of the garden. Make major level changes, if necessary, and fix the position of the paths and patio, greenhouse and cold frames, even if you can't construct them yet. Provide boundaries, if none exist, for security and privacy.

Give priority to establishing large, long-term plants, such as trees, followed by shrubs and climbers and finally, perennials, bulbs and annuals.

A few trays of bedding plants can brighten up a first-year garden at very little cost, and it doesn't matter where you put them, as they only last one season. Large flower pots and tubs are always useful, as they can be instantly filled with plants and moved around to wherever colour is needed.

Ornamental features such as pools, rockeries and pergolas can be constructed after the main planting and garden framework are established – but remember to leave space for them.

▼ **Small and perfect** However well planned, a garden develops gradually and only as plants mature and fill out do the creative merits of the design become obvious.

PLANTING A GARDEN

Creative garden designs succeed in using plants to maintain colour and focal interest throughout the twelve months of the year.

Many new gardeners concentrate their efforts and budget into a colourful summer display and forget about the other nine months of the year. A successful garden design will use plants for year-round effect, creating areas of seasonal interest and relying on permanent and evergreen groups to keep the garden alive when herbaceous plants have long died down for their winter rest.

A balance of plants

The garden featured on the following pages shows how to enjoy a summer crescendo of colour and still have plenty of interest during the rest of the year.

The garden is west-facing and therefore has summer sun nearly all day long; gardens with less favourable aspects can be equally stunning for many bedding plants do well in dappled shade.

The recipe for success throughout the year is simple and can be applied to any garden: include a balance of plants.

Mix seasonal, short-lived plants with permanent trees and shrubs; deciduous with evergreen; flowers with foliage; strong colours with green or similar soothing hues; and 'soft' planting with well-placed focal points.

Seasonal planting

Ringing the changes with seasonal planting is a popular gardening pastime, and many people spend the winter months browsing

▲ **Summer highlights** This mature garden uses borders of shrubs and foliage plants as props for a velvety lawn and island beds of brilliant colours.

▼ **Raised beds** Level changes in steps and raised beds brimming with colour-co-ordinated, upright, trailing and climbing plants bring a three-dimensional feel to the paved patio.

through seed catalogues, choosing new varieties and colours.

Growing your own bedding plants from seed is economical – particularly if you are planning a display on the scale of this garden – but you can find yourself swamped with unwanted plants.

If you only need a relatively small number of plants, buy them ready grown in late spring. Larger garden centres always feature a few new varieties among the traditional ones.

Raised beds Bedding plants are set out in raised beds built into the patio, each bed with its own colour theme and particular plants and patterns. One bed, for example, is based on pink petunias, blue lobelia and white alyssum; another, on red-purple lobelia, yellow bedding calceolarias, white alyssum and pink geraniums.

Containers on the patio also have their own colour themes. Bright red begonias, both tuberous-rooted and wax varieties, fill the two-level stone container, and a mixture of trailing fuchsias, geraniums, *Helichrysum petiolatum*, alyssum and lobelia fill urns and planting troughs.

Two island beds in the lawn are filled with more fuchsias – shrubby types for bulk and standards for height. The beds are edged with busy Lizzies and begonias, in shades of red.

Every autumn, beds and containers are cleared and prepared for the following spring display. The fuchsias are dug up and overwintered in a frost-free greenhouse. The tuberous-rooted begonias are lifted, dried off and overwintered in boxes of dry compost.

Cuttings are taken from the geraniums to supply the next summer's plants, and annuals are put on the compost heap to rot down to compost which can be returned to the soil with much of the nutrients they took out.

Spring bedding includes a large number of tulips and daffodils. This is less extravagant than it sounds, since bulbs will last for decades if properly looked after. Early in the summer, when flowering has finished, they are lifted, cleaned and dried off, then replanted during the autumn. You could leave daffodils and narcissi in the ground to naturalize, but bedding tulips are best lifted and stored annually.

Young bulbils produced by the parent bulbs are left to grow on in a spare patch of land for two or three years until they are big enough to flower, so the numbers increase freely.

Biennials, such as wallflowers, pansies, forget-me-nots, sweet Williams, polyanthus and double daisies, are planted out in autumn. Again, they are grown from seed and arranged in patterns and colour themes which change from year to year. The polyanthus, pansies and double daisies give double value, as they often flower from autumn onwards.

Permanent planting

Adequate space is given to long-term residents – trees, shrubs and a choice of conifers – which provide the permanent backdrop to the changing spring and summer displays. They reduce considerably the amount of maintenance needed to keep the garden looking good at all times.

One of the three island beds is planted with evergreens – heathers, pines and junipers – and the large rockery that runs along one

◄ **Conifers for height** Mature cypresses at the back of the garden lift the view from the level plane. In winter, the group becomes a dramatic focal point, the golden conifer bright on the dullest day.

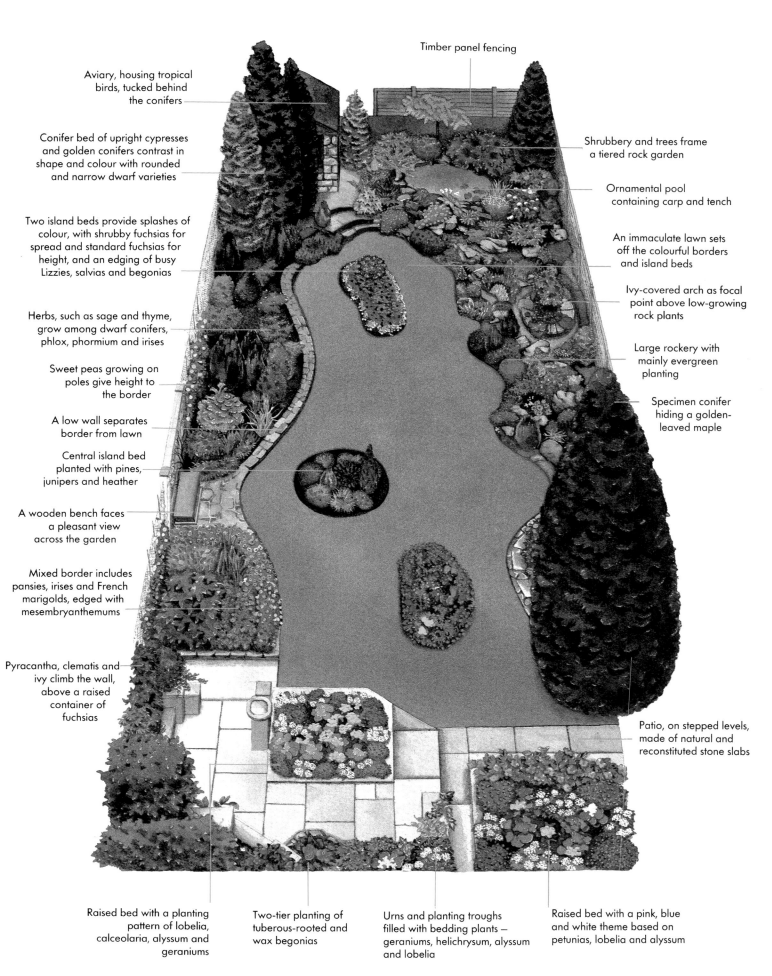

Timber panel fencing

Aviary, housing tropical birds, tucked behind the conifers

Conifer bed of upright cypresses and golden conifers contrast in shape and colour with rounded and narrow dwarf varieties

Two island beds provide splashes of colour, with shrubby fuchsias for spread and standard fuchsias for height, and an edging of busy Lizzies, salvias and begonias

Herbs, such as sage and thyme, grow among dwarf conifers, phlox, phormium and irises

Sweet peas growing on poles give height to the border

A low wall separates border from lawn

Central island bed planted with pines, junipers and heather

A wooden bench faces a pleasant view across the garden

Mixed border includes pansies, irises and French marigolds, edged with mesembryanthemums

Pyracantha, clematis and ivy climb the wall, above a raised container of fuchsias

Shrubbery and trees frame a tiered rock garden

Ornamental pool containing carp and tench

An immaculate lawn sets off the colourful borders and island beds

Ivy-covered arch as focal point above low-growing rock plants

Large rockery with mainly evergreen planting

Specimen conifer hiding a golden-leaved maple

Patio, on stepped levels, made of natural and reconstituted stone slabs

Raised bed with a planting pattern of lobelia, calceolaria, alyssum and geraniums

Two-tier planting of tuberous-rooted and wax begonias

Urns and planting troughs filled with bedding plants — geraniums, helichrysum, alyssum and lobelia

Raised bed with a pink, blue and white theme based on petunias, lobelia and alyssum

HOUSE

side of the garden is planted with evergreen sempervivums and hebes, and numerous conifers in a range of foliage colours and shapes that vary from miniature and ground-hugging to columnar exclamation marks for added height.

The use of tall, narrow conifers of various heights sets up a rhythm throughout the garden. Upright planting contrasts effectively with the more rounded forms of other conifers and low-growing shrubs, such as hebes and rock roses.

A selection of heathers, including winter-flowering types, acts as year-round ground cover, visually weaving together the conifers. Evergreen rhododendrons provide colourful spring flowers. Autumn leaf colour, and more spring flowers, come from azaleas (*Rhododendron mollis* varieties), while maples add height, brilliant autumn colour and attractive bare winter branches.

◄ **Bedding plants** A half-hardy, standard trained fuchsia rises above a froth of busy Lizzies and tuberous begonias. The neat edging of green and bronze-leaved wax begonias repeats the pink and red colour theme.

THE ROCK GARDEN

The rockery is planted with a mass of mainly evergreen species. The plan helps to identify the plants opposite.

1 Maiden pink (*Dianthus deltoides*)
2 Heather (*Calluna vulgaris*)
3 Shrubby veronica (*Hebe albicans*)
4 Houseleek (*Sempervivum*)
5 Rock phlox (*Phlox subulata*)
6 Rock rose (*Helianthemum nummularium*)
7 Fuchsia 'Tom Thumb'
8 Bearberry (*Arctostaphylos uva-ursi*)
9 Dwarf juniper (*Juniperus communis*)
10 Japanese cedar (*Cryptomeria japonica*)
11 *Thujopsis dolabrata*
12 Dwarf blue spruce (*Picea pungens*)
13 Dwarf Californian redwood (*Sequoia sempervirens* 'Adpressa')

14 Dwarf juniper (*Juniperus × media*)
15 Dwarf Lawson's cypress (*Chamaecyparis lawsoniana*)
16 Stonecrop (*Sedum acre*)
17 *Alyssum saxatile*
18 Knotweed (*Polygonum affine*)
19 Coral flower (*Heuchera sanguinea*)
20 Dwarf Hinoki cypress (*Chamaecyparis obtusa*)
21 *Thuja occidentalis*
22 *Rhododendron* hybrid
23 *Hydrangea macrophylla*
24 *Phlox paniculata*
25 Ivy (*Hedera canariensis* 'Variegata')
26 Blue Atlas cedar (*Cedrus atlantica* 'Glauca')
27 Cucumber tree (*Magnolia acuminata*)
28 Purple-leaved plum (*Prunus cerasifera* 'Pissardii')

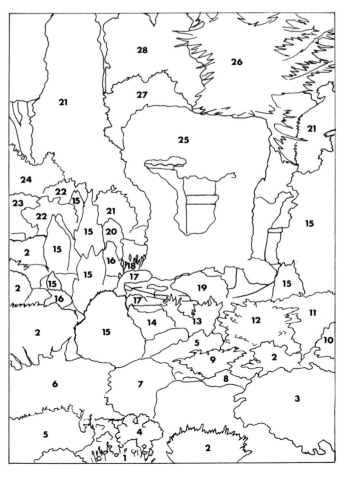

Snowdrops and crocuses give winter and early spring interest. They are planted in pockets in the rockery and come up year after year, gradually spreading to form wide clumps.

The lawn

The immaculate lawn needs care and attention, but the end result is worth the regular mowing, feeding and edge-trimming required. The velvety carpet provides a restful contrast with the more colourful beds and borders. The stripes echo the curves of flower beds and borders, as well as the shape of the garden.

Design features

The hard features in this garden comprise patio, rockery, bench and decorative wall, the ivy-covered arch, pools, rock garden, and aviary at the back. These have all been added over the years, but were included in the original garden plan to avoid major alterations to established planting schemes.

The patio, as useful as it is ornamental, overlooks the whole of the garden, and is made of a mixture of stone materials.

At the far end of the garden is an aviary. In its place you could consider constructing a toolshed or a greenhouse. Alternatively, you could use the space to create a small vegetable plot.

▲ **Sunny retreat** A wooden bench on concrete supports is set between the two sweeping curves of the mixed border and looks across an island bed, to the pool and rockery beyond.

The wall behind ensures privacy and shelter, and the perforated concrete blocks and multi-coloured stonework add a decorative touch.

Island beds are set well inside the lawn so as to make mowing easy. Narrow strips of lawn are difficult to keep clipped. The edges tend to crumble and cave in if subjected to the wear and tear of a lawnmower.

Equally practical is the low walling along the mixed border. It keeps the lawn well and truly separated from the border and prevents any grass straying from one to the other.

▶ **Focal points** Near the patio is an ornamental pool, its still surface almost hidden in summer by the glossy floating leaves and brilliant blooms of hardy water lilies.

Designs for small gardens

A well-designed small garden minimizes the restrictions imposed by limited space and essentially becomes an extension of the house, an outdoor living room. A small garden is usually sheltered and can be turned into an inward-looking and secluded place for relaxation. Any disadvantages incurred by its size are outweighed by the corresponding ease with which it can be maintained.

Small gardens are often awkward shapes – long and narrow or squat and box-like – but good design ideas can alter the perspective. Changes in level can be visually deceptive, as well as increasing the space for growing plants, and curving lines can lead the eye on a circuitous rather than a straight and narrow route.

Hard landscape features are especially important in small gardens which permit no outside views; they often have to replace a conventional lawn and can open up numerous design possibilities, from courtyard gardens and basement pools to miniscule front gardens.

Planting is of necessity restricted and, therefore, requires extra careful consideration. It should be profuse enough to create a feeling of seclusion yet avoid a cluttered look. Front gardens are often the most challenging to design, but even the smallest space has enough potential to express its owner's personality.

Visual appeal Old-fashioned charm is evident in a cottage-garden approach with pot marigolds and poppies.

FIRST IMPRESSIONS

**A fine front garden makes a fitting entrance
to a home. Even the smallest of plots has the potential
to create a welcoming first impression.**

However lovely your home is on the inside, the outside is seen first. Whether it's for passers-by, family or guests, most people like their homes to look welcoming from the start, and to reveal a bit of personal style. An attractive exterior is also an investment, enhancing a property's value.

Obviously, the larger the front garden, the greater the possibilities. But even if your garden is minute, there is usually room for pot plants and greenery.

A pocket-handkerchief garden can hold surprisingly large plants. And because there may be room for only one or two shrubs, you can buy extra large specimen plants for instant impact.

The soil in a tiny plot – particularly in towns – may be worn out, compacted and sour. It's worth buying bags of prepared planting compost and soil-based loam to enrich or replace poor soil.

Setting the tone
If possible, respond to the architectural style, mood and scale of the house. A fine exterior, such as a well-proportioned Georgian façade, needs very little planting to emphasize its good points, while a house with little character might well benefit from an evergreen camouflage.

Plants and containers don't have to be historically accurate in relation to the house style, but they shouldn't look out of place.

Attention to detail is important since a single window-box or tub becomes an immediate focal point.

▼ **Warm welcome** A magnificent mophead hydrangea by a bright red front door creates a cheerful impression. By the autumn, the dead flower heads turn russet-brown and continue to look attractive through winter.

▲ Climbing roses Fragrant climbers of the repeat-flowering type provide a sweet-scented greeting of gorgeous blooms through the summer. The yellow 'Casino' and the pink 'Compassion' have a particularly heady scent. But roses need tying in, pruning and dead-heading and in winter they can look gaunt. An evergreen honeysuckle could be planted as a companion for year-round cover and extra fragrance.

► Front door elegance A single stone tub matches the classic simplicity of this front entrance. Planted with evergreen bay and a footing of small-leaved ivy, it takes spring colour from daffodils and polyanthus primroses. The colour scheme echoes that of the window-box.

Versailles planters enhance the formality of classical façades, wooden half barrels suit the cottage style, and simple terracotta pots suit anything. Containers with grand aspirations, such as elaborate stone urns, rarely look at ease in modest settings.

Most plants can be used formally or informally, but some plants set a particular style. Topiary box and bay convey formality while rampant honeysuckle does the opposite. This doesn't have to limit choice – cottage gardens have a splendid mix of formal and informal plants.

Front doors and porches

Many Georgian, Regency and Victorian terraces and modern town houses have façades directly fronting the pavement, with one or more steps up to the front door.

Where space allows, a tub or large flower pot is attractive. One good-sized evergreen shrub – bay, box, fatsia, camellia or aucuba – makes a better impression than many little plants, and bulbs and annuals can be added for seasonal interest and colour.

A pair of tubs supporting the symmetry of a classical front door is impressive. If the entrance is narrow, vertically trained bays or slim conifers are ideal.

Front-door tubs or pots for specimen plants should be at least 30cm (1ft) wide to look effective, retain moisture and withstand knocks without toppling. If necessary, raise large containers on bricks for drainage; chain the containers to a wall or railings if they might be stolen.

Some houses have several steps up to the front door. If width allows, a row of flower pots can line one or both sides of the steps. Again, make sure they are secure, both for their wellbeing and for safety. Large pots could be tucked in the corner of the steps and house walls, and climbers trained up and along any railings.

Climbers supported by sturdy trellis or vine eyes and wires can be trained around a front door, open-fronted porch or portico.

House walls

Before choosing a climbing plant for a house wall, decide just what effect you want to create. Some climbing plants, such as Virginia creeper, will cover an entire wall; others produce lovely flowers.

▲ **Romantic wisteria** The dream of a country cottage always includes a climber scrambling over white-washed walls. Here, a wisteria has been trained along strong wires to frame windows and door. Its rambling growth is kept within bounds by judicious pruning in winter and summer.

▶ **Topiary sentinels** A fine exterior needs few decorative touches. Small-leaved box, clipped into spheres, emphasize this handsome front door. Such restrained elegance suits houses directly fronting a pavement.

Consider combining different plants – perhaps clematis and evergreen honeysuckle – for year-round value.

Remember, many climbers need supports, and some climb rampantly – pruning could present problems if the house wall is high.

Be careful with self-clinging climbers, such as ivy, which can penetrate old mortar. On painted walls, the choice is limited to plants that can be released and laid along the ground during painting and then retied in place.

Certain shrubs can be trained against a wall. Pyracantha and ceanothus are useful evergreen wall shrubs, and chaenomeles gives an early show of flowers.

Aspect is important. Plants that thrive by a south-facing wall may

fail to perform in shade. Wall-trained plants benefit from the shelter and latent warmth so you could try slightly tender types, such as the passion flower or climbing pineapple-scented broom (*Cytisus battandieri*).

Window-boxes, hanging baskets and wall-hung half baskets can be fixed to a front façade. Wall-hung plants are most effective clustered near the door or window at eye-level height or just below, though a high hanging basket filled with trailing plants is enchanting. Make sure containers can be easily reached for watering.

Balconies range from window ledges with railings to generous walk-on terraces. Plants can trail or grow upwards to cover an area far greater than the balcony size. The higher a balcony is, the more exposed it may be, so delicate plants may be unsuitable.

Weight is an important factor, especially if the balcony is cantilevered. Get professional advice if you want large containers.

If there is a basement area, consider planting a tall-growing climber such as Boston ivy or wisteria or a vigorous shrub, for example evergreen magnolia, for training up the front façade.

Minute gardens

The smaller the garden, the simpler the layout should be. Attractive paving with a single

▲ **Old-world charm** A small cottage garden is a mass of summer colours from old-fashioned favourites — senecios, campanulas, roses and potentillas. Centrepiece of the tiny, gravel-covered front garden is an urn filled with catmint (*Nepeta* × *faassenii*).

pot-grown specimen shrub is often more attractive than a minuscule lawn. A gravel surface studded with clipped box or bay, or a multi-stemmed fig is also effective in a small plot.

It is important to respect the general mood of neighbouring gardens. Nothing looks more inappropriate than one house in a terrace that breaks the rhythm or established pattern of all the others.

▼ **Modern cottage garden** This alternative to the garden shown opposite is planted for interest through the year. Senecio remains, and summer jasmine by the house wall continues to waft fragrance through the air. Colours are gentle, mainly greens and gold, with an emphasis on attractive leaf form

In one corner behind a yellow-flowered *Crocosmia* 'Citronella', is the soft green foliage of white-flowered *Philadelphus* 'Beauclerk'. The yellow spikes of *Verbascum* 'Gainsborough' contrast with *Rosa* 'Golden Wings'

Foliage plants include hostas, golden marjoram and *Stachys lanata* — the unusual, green-leaved *Stachys olympica* 'Primrose Heron' (shown) is particularly effective. Yellow Welsh poppies (*Meconopsis cambrica*) are encouraged to self-seed around the garden

Screening the boundary is the autumn yellow-berried firethorn, *Pyracantha* 'Soleil d'Or'. In front, the dwarf *Thuja occidentalis* 'Woodwardii' forms a dense globe of rich green

Fronting the plot is a double row of shrubs. *Spiraea japonica* 'Golden Dome' fronts the prickly evergreen *Berberis stenophylla* 'Cream Showers' to make an informal low hedge

Evergreens like *Juniperus communis* 'Depressa Aurea' give a lovely golden glow. Also of value in winter is the summer-flowering *Hypericum* 'Hidcote' which retains its leaves

▲ **Flowering hedges** In spring forsythia bursts into glorious golden bloom lasting for several weeks. It quickly forms a dense hedge from rooted cuttings planted 30cm (1ft) apart, and it responds well to clipping. Do not prune after early summer or you will cut off the flower buds for next year's display.

► **Fragrant lavender** Popular for path edging since the Middle Ages, lavender, in shades of blue, pink and pure white, fills the air with its sweet scent on long summer days. Cut the faded flower stems back in late summer and prune back hard in spring to avoid the plants becoming leggy.

▲ **Roses all the way** A low picket fence supports the free-flowering climbing rose 'American Pillar' in New England style. On the house wall, a vigorous rambling rose, the white 'Félicité et Perpétue' adds to the rustic charm.

◄ **Town house style** This tiny front garden perfectly complements the house. It is contained within a low wall, rendered and painted to match the house walls, and is topped with decorative railings that add height without throwing shade. A pair of standard roses and the white-painted trellis also help to lift the view from the level plane.

◄ **Front garden** Suburban gardens are often conventional in style, with a straight path, borders and a specimen tree or shrub. The choice of plants, however, can change a garden from the ordinary to the outstanding.

Here, two focal points near the boundary immediately attract the eye. By the house is a purple-leaved cherry plum (*Prunus cerasifera* 'Pissardii') that is a mass of blooms in spring, and near the front hedge of golden privet is a smoke tree (*Cotinus coggygria*) whose feathery purple-hazy flower clusters in summer are matched by brilliant autumn colours.

A white climbing rose, 'Iceberg', and an ornamental vine with rich autumn tints embellish the walls.

► **Town garden** The brick edging round the flagstone centre blends well with the house, and strong plant shapes make a memorable first impression.

The symmetrical design is accentuated with a low lavender hedge and with stone urns containing dwarf cypresses. Year-round colour comes from other evergreens — mahonias, Portuguese laurel, clipped senecios in beds by the windows and a neat box hedge behind ornamental railings.

The house wall is draped with wisteria, but pride of place goes to a magnificent evergreen *Magnolia grandiflora*.

◄ **Open-plan garden** Many front gardens on large estates are without boundary divisions. This garden was planned for individual character while retaining the open aspect.

Irregular-shaped beds set into the lawn are planted with ground-hugging shrubs and perennials — including hosta, lady's mantle and bergenias — all with attractive leaves.

The specimen tree is a graceful weeping silver pear (*Pyrus salicifolia*). Clipped bay standards flank the front door, and pyracantha is trained against the house wall. A curving path helps to disguise the outline of the linear plot.

LONG AND NARROW GARDENS

Creative design ideas can release a garden from a regimented appearance and turn it into a pleasant outdoor living room for the family.

The majority of gardens are created along straight lines, sometimes square and box-like but more often long and narrow. They are hemmed in by straight boundaries and accentuated with fences and hedges. Much garden design follows this linear outline instead of releasing it from the strait-jacket with curving lines that visually deceive the eye by introducing false perspectives, perhaps to cleverly placed focal points.

Traditionally, a path leads from the house to the bottom of the garden. In long gardens, this has the effect of cutting the plot into two narrow strips that further emphasize the outline. A path, when necessary, does not have to follow a straight line down the middle but can curve along one side so as to make the garden look wider; flowing rather than straight lines to the lawn will have the same effect. The borders thus created will vary in depth and therefore allow more interesting and varied planting schemes to be designed.

Garden divisions

Long, narrow gardens such as the one featured here are a definite challenge. The object is to soften and conceal the narrow proportions and this has been achieved by dividing the garden into a series of simple areas, each following on from the next in a smoothly flowing design, and each stretching across the entire width. Within the garden's divisions, there's plenty of scope to include elements that meet the whole family's needs.

The first division is the two-level patio, followed by the lawn and finally the back area, which is laid with crazy paving and entered through the pergola. The wide, shrub-filled borders on either side of

the pergola create a narrow entrance-way and, because they partially obscure the back of the garden, add an element of mystery. You can imagine the garden extending well beyond its actual boundary.

A family garden

The divisions in this garden are both practical and attractive, and suit children and adults alike.

There is a swing for the children and, more importantly, a good-sized lawn and patio for playing on. A family garden that has 'no go' areas for children can be a constant source of friction and, however beautiful, is usually not worth the trouble.

Adults find the patio and lawn equally pleasurable, both to look at and to use. The patio is ideal for entertaining, whether a full-

▶ **Visual deception** The long, narrow outline of this garden has disappeared. The new design has introduced curves along the boundaries and changes in level near the house, creating separate areas for different activities yet maintaining unity and harmony.

▲ Patio and steps A bird's eye view of the two-level patio and wide shallow steps with groups of container plants.

scale barbecue or afternoon tea, or simply sitting out – although the garden faces north, the house is low enough for the sun to reach most areas for most of the day in summer. The barbecue and adjacent table are conveniently near to the house, and the barbecue is portable for easy storage.

The flower beds contain a range of vegetables, such as runner beans, mingling with the flowers, and plenty of shrubs for winter interest. A few well placed trees add height, but are not so high that they overshadow the garden.

A gently curving hexagon path leads the eye (as well as the feet) to the white-painted pergola. This half conceals the small greenhouse behind. Finishing touches include low raised planting beds and numerous container plants, which add splashes of colour to the scene.

Level changes

A garden with level changes is visually more attractive than one on a level plane. It gives an impression of enclosure, shelter and privacy on low-lying ground and a sense of opening out where the level rises. This low-level patio takes on the feeling of a room, but very much a room with a view. The house walls shield the patio further, while the generously wide steps beckon the eye to admire the garden beyond.

The steps Apart from connecting

▼ Barbecue area Safely away from general garden traffic, the barbecue becomes a natural focal point in summer. Plants in pots and planting pockets enliven the area without turning the steps into an obstacle course.

the upper and lower garden levels, the steps provide extra informal seating, for children who rarely use garden seats, given half a chance to sit elsewhere. The steps also provide space for setting out seasonal displays of pot plants.

The pot-plant theme is repeated on the patio itself and, Mediterranean style, as a wall-hung planting display high enough above the barbecue not to be singed. Hard surfaces, whether horizontal or vertical, make an excellent setting for plants, and both benefit visually. The plants' natural beauty and irregular growth soften harsh materials and hard geometry, and the plain background of concrete, brick or stone shows up and enhances individual plants in a way that is rarely possible in mixed beds or borders.

The patio is paved in concrete slabs coloured and moulded to look like old-fashioned granite setts. Two patterns – straight rows of setts and quarter circles – are laid imaginatively to create a semi-abstract pattern. Another approach would be to lay a series of four quarter-circle slabs together, to create several large 'granite sett' circular patterns. Other options using concrete include slabs dyed and textured to look either like natural stone or

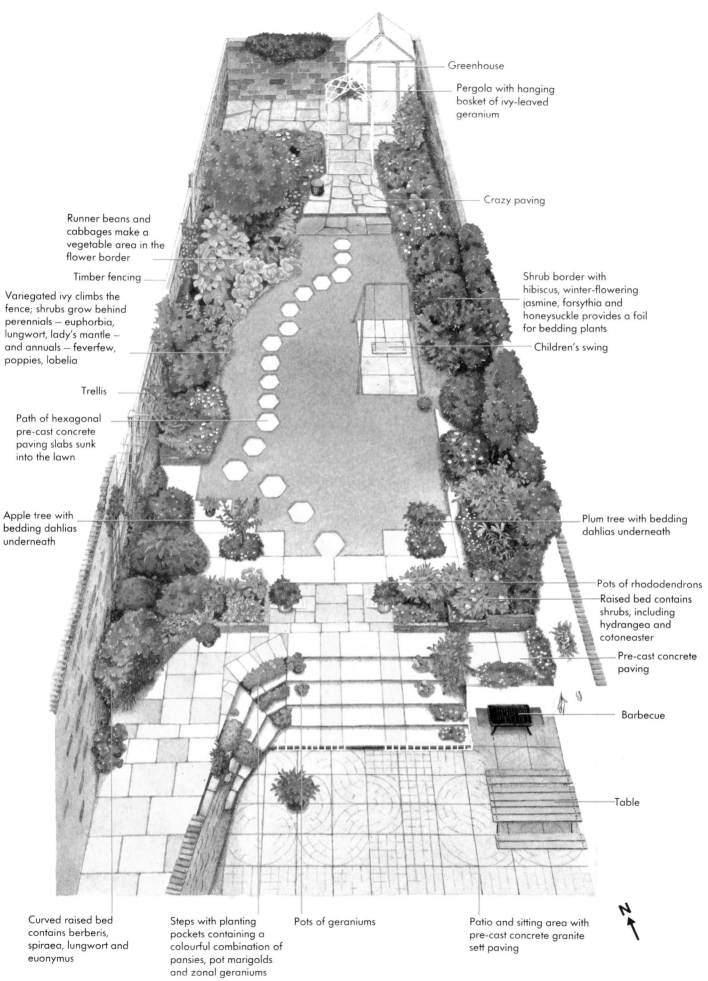

Greenhouse

Pergola with hanging basket of ivy-leaved geranium

Runner beans and cabbages make a vegetable area in the flower border

Crazy paving

Timber fencing

Variegated ivy climbs the fence; shrubs grow behind perennials — euphorbia, lungwort, lady's mantle — and annuals — feverfew, poppies, lobelia

Shrub border with hibiscus, winter-flowering jasmine, forsythia and honeysuckle provides a foil for bedding plants

Children's swing

Trellis

Path of hexagonal pre-cast concrete paving slabs sunk into the lawn

Apple tree with bedding dahlias underneath

Plum tree with bedding dahlias underneath

Pots of rhododendrons

Raised bed contains shrubs, including hydrangea and cotoneaster

Pre-cast concrete paving

Barbecue

Table

Curved raised bed contains berberis, spiraea, lungwort and euonymus

Steps with planting pockets containing a colourful combination of pansies, pot marigolds and zonal geraniums

Pots of geraniums

Patio and sitting area with pre-cast concrete granite sett paving

N

HOUSE

▲ **Spotted lungwort** Also known as Bethlehem sage, *Pulmonaria saccharata* relishes shade. Its large silver-marbled leaves provide year-round ground cover, enlivened in spring with pink and blue flower clusters and later with the bright yellow of annual pot marigolds (*Calendula officinalis*) and the lime-green feathery sprays of lady's mantle.

▶ **Curving path** Hexagonal pre-cast paving slabs are set just below the lawn level for easy mowing. The line follows the curved edge of the border from the upper patio with its planting pockets and raised beds to the paved service area and greenhouse at the end of the garden.

rows of bricks. Of course, if finances run to it, you could use the real thing.

The steps and upper garden immediately surrounding the patio are paved in simple concrete slabs, of varied size and colour. Paving and lawn interlock in a staggered pattern – a more unusual approach than a straight line.

Another blend of 'soft' and 'hard' landscape is the series of planting pockets in the corner of the steps, where the change to retaining wall begins. Here, foliage plants minimize the need for tricky slab cutting, and become a focal point. **The raised flower beds** on the upper patio create a third level change. Permanent planting and colourful annuals spill over the low brick walls, making a gateway of greenery into the garden proper. The gateway idea is repeated in the bright white miniature fencing that spans both the lower and upper paved areas.

An alternative design

This alternative plan (see page 50) for a long narrow garden contains the same elements – lawn, patio, barbecue, greenhouse, flowers, shrubs, trees and vegetables, and somewhere for the children to play – but put together in a less ambitious design. The linear outline has been retained, but by dividing the garden into compartments it looks shorter and wider.

Paving A theme of brick and plain concrete slabs is used for all hard surfaces, with one large planting bed marking the transition from patio and surrounds to the garden proper. The rectangular, uncluttered lawn extends from the fence to the path that runs along a narrow border. A neatly clipped yew hedge hides the vegetable garden and service area with greenhouse from general view.

The garden is easy to maintain, with plenty of scope for recreation and relaxation.

A sand-pit is situated within sight of the house and patio. At a later stage it can easily be converted into an ornamental pool or a rock garden.

◄ **Mixed border** Cropping plants such as scarlet-flowered runner beans are grown among ornamentals in the wide curving border. Other tall-growing plants include the late-summer flowering golden rod (*Solidago* × *hybrida*), with spotted lungwort and nasturtiums spilling over the edge.

▼ **Raised bed** Close to the patio, a raised bed planted with tall-growing shrubs and climbers ensures privacy from the neighbouring house. A honeysuckle (*Lonicera japonica*) trained along the fence adds fragrance above clumps of lilies. White achilleas and yellow loosestrife (*Lysimachia punctata*) contrast well with pots of rich blue trailing lobelia.

► **Pergolas**
These come in a range of styles and materials to suit all types of gardens. Painted pergolas, like the one on the right, need regular maintenance.

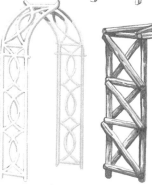

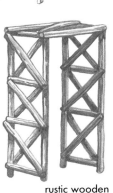

ornamental iron   rustic wooden

ALTERNATIVE DESIGN

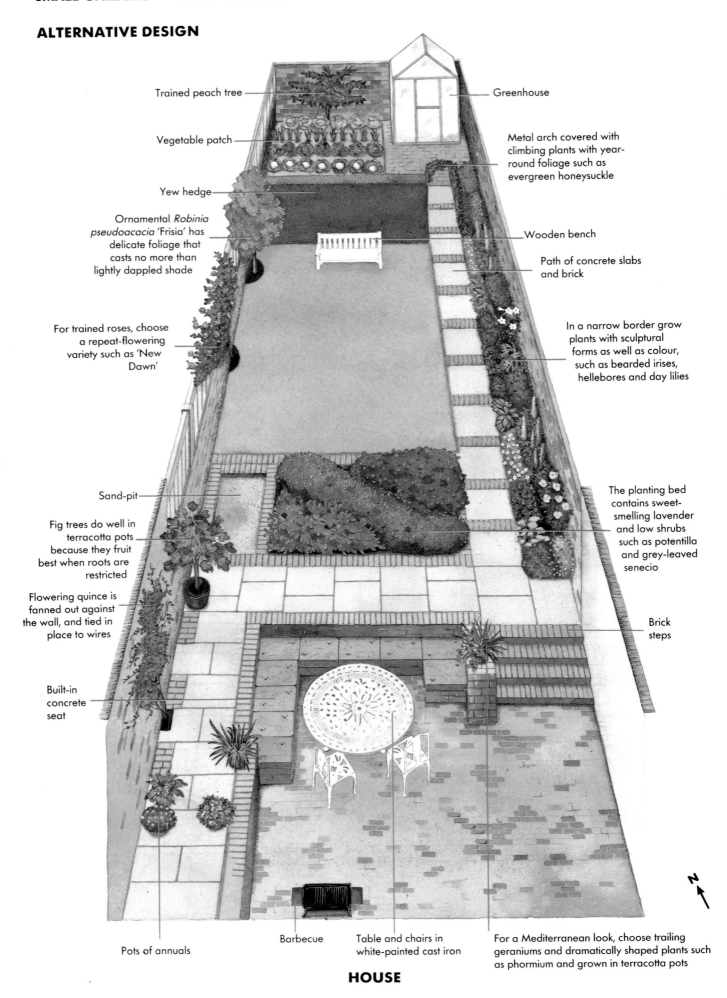

Trained peach tree

Greenhouse

Vegetable patch

Metal arch covered with climbing plants with year-round foliage such as evergreen honeysuckle

Yew hedge

Ornamental *Robinia pseudoacacia* 'Frisia' has delicate foliage that casts no more than lightly dappled shade

Wooden bench

Path of concrete slabs and brick

For trained roses, choose a repeat-flowering variety such as 'New Dawn'

In a narrow border grow plants with sculptural forms as well as colour, such as bearded irises, hellebores and day lilies

Sand-pit

Fig trees do well in terracotta pots because they fruit best when roots are restricted

The planting bed contains sweet-smelling lavender and low shrubs such as potentilla and grey-leaved senecio

Flowering quince is fanned out against the wall, and tied in place to wires

Brick steps

Built-in concrete seat

Pots of annuals

Barbecue

Table and chairs in white-painted cast iron

For a Mediterranean look, choose trailing geraniums and dramatically shaped plants such as phormium and grown in terracotta pots

HOUSE

BOX-SHAPED GARDENS

**A simple, crisp design and inspired planting
have helped to transform a small rectangular plot
into an elegant town garden.**

When faced with a rectangular plot the first instinct of many gardeners is to counteract the geometry with curves: curved paths, lawns, beds, borders and even circular ornamental pools.

This is often attractive, but a garden that turns the limitations of a rectangular layout into a positive design feature can also be appealing. There is something very crisp and refreshing about a garden that retains its right-angled geometry.

The key to success is simplicity: a clean, bold layout, and good quality but plain hard landscaping materials. Straight lines can be softened by dense, informal planting.

Though this garden has the benefit of mature trees and shrubs, hard landscaping in a new garden can be effectively softened with quick-growing annuals, climbers and perennials until slower growing woody plants begin to make an impact.

The site and layout

The rectangular level plot is the back garden of a town house. A large paved area extends from the back of the house roughly to the middle of the garden, and is surrounded on three sides by a low stone retaining wall. Behind the wall are raised planting beds and – the main feature of the garden – a large raised L-shaped pool.

The overall effect is one of plea-

▼ **Spring colour** Lily-flowered tulips – 'China Pink', yellow 'West Point' and 'White Triumphator' – seem all the more spectacular viewed against a backdrop of foliage and reflected in the still water of the pool.

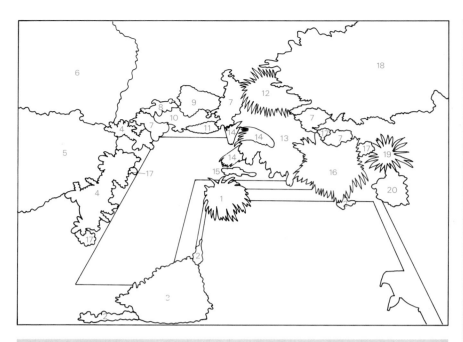

SUMMER SCENE

Boundary greenery — some borrowed from neighbouring gardens — forms a backdrop to enclose this elegant town garden. The plan shown above identifies the main planting on the right.

1 Kaffir lily (*Clivia miniata*)
2 Common ivy (*Hedera helix*)
3 Goldfish plant (*Columnea*)
4 *Mahonia nervosa*
5 Privet (*Ligustrum ovalifolium*)
6 *Magnolia grandiflora*
7 *Senecio clivorum*
8 *Hosta* 'Royal Standard'
9 Dwarf bamboo (*Arundinaria humilis*)
10 Lady fern (*Athyrium filix-femina*)
11 Sweet woodruff (*Galium odoratum*)
12 Feather grass (*Stipa gigantea*)
13 Arrowhead (*Sagittaria* species)
14 Reedmace (*Typha miniata*)
15 Miniature water lily (*Nymphaea* hybrid)
16 Fountain grass (*Pennisetum orientale*)
17 Busy Lizzie (*Impatiens wallerana*)
18 Chinese privet (*Ligustrum lucidum*)
19 *Yucca gloriosa*
20 Chinese hibiscus (*Hibiscus rosa-sinensis*)

sant enclosure, reinforced by tall perimeter planting beyond. Access from the house is through French doors flanked by tall vertical glass panels and topped with a huge, semi-circular window – an impressive feature seen from the garden.

At first-floor level, a roof terrace, complete with table and chairs, overlooks the garden, which is the focal point for the terrace and the living room.

Having mature gardens on all sides, the garden benefits from borrowed landscape – notably a magnificent mature evergreen magnolia growing in an adjacent garden but overhanging the pool.

Other neighbouring shrubs and trees help to create a sense of high-level enclosure, kept comfortably open at ground level by the broad expanse of paving and water. The neighbouring shrubs and trees also confuse the garden's boundaries, making the plot seem larger than it actually is.

Hard landscaping

The hard landscaping is attractive, sturdy and unpretentious. Large rectangular riven slate paving slabs are laid in straight rows, with tightly butted open joints and staggered cross joints.

Minor variation in tone, from cool to rosy greys, and natural variation in surface texture create quiet, subtle patterns.

The raised pool wall continues the natural stone theme, the irregularly shaped stones contrasting in scale and texture with the larger slate slabs. The wall varies in construction from tight, parallel courses to a more random effect, rather like vertical crazy paving.

The flat stone coping on top of the pool wall emphasizes the formal geometry, and its pale tone makes the water seem darker and more mysterious by comparison. The coping provides extra seating and a vantage point from which to view the goldfish.

An old brick wall forms one long garden boundary; vertical, close-boarded wood panels form the rest. Both have weathered to soft tones,

General planting

The silvery grey wood a variation on the grey of the paving.

The planting is mixed in the best sense of the word: bright splashes of seasonal colour coming from popular, easily available plants – bulbs, for example – set against a background of permanent trees and shrubs, including a good pro-portion of evergreen varieties for winter cover.

Though not a purely foliage gar-den – flowers are included, and many of the plants have un-memorable leaves – there is enough outstanding foliage to make an overall impact. Varie-gated and non-green foliage are deliberately excluded to provide a completely restful background for bursts of colour from the flowers.

Variation, instead, comes from scale and form: huge round leaves, lacy fronds, and grassy, upright or arching foliage, itself contrasting with the strong horizontal planes of the paving and water.

A large, multi-stemmed Chinese privet punctuates one end of the pool, and huge hollies form a dense screen at the back of the garden.

◄ **Focal point** The L-shaped pool is the dominant feature in this small garden. It is framed by pleasing greenery from mature trees and shrubs that give a sense of secluded enclosure. Round the pool grow moisture lovers such as hostas, ferns and bamboos above a ground cover of sweet woodruff; the pool itself is stocked with reedmace, large-leaved arrowheads and baskets of water lilies.

▼ **Fountains and water** From a raised bed, a huge mound of fountain grass (*Pennisetum orientale*) arches its foliage and soft, catkin-like seed heads over the pool edge. It breaks up the severe lines of the coping and contrasts in form and texture with a nearby spiky yucca.

In a long, narrow planting bed next to the pool, a row of evergreen mahonias creates a solid barrier, with whorls of leaves at slightly different heights and angles setting up a pleasing rhythm.

Where the raised beds widen there are laurels, kalmias and evergreen honeysuckle (*Lonicera fragrantissima*). Ivy is used as a climber and for ground cover, even gaining a foothold in the narrow joints between paving and wall.

Red and yellow flowers predominate; grouped in large masses, they are surrounded by dense greenery. As well as red, yellow, pink and white tulips – all planted in broad beds of single colours – there are daffodils and forget-me-nots for an early show.

By the time the spring display finishes and bulbs are lifted or die back, herbaceous perennials have taken over, hiding the ground and giving new colour.

SECLUDED GARDENS

**Many gardens lack privacy, but with an
imaginative design and bold planting, a garden
can become a haven of tranquillity.**

Seclusion is an important element in most gardens and there are several ways of creating your own private haven. The garden featured here is especially well planned with excellent design qualities that provide several good ideas to help you to achieve this kind of intimacy.

Brick walls can play a vital role. They act as a good sound barrier by minimizing noise from traffic and neighbours; they effectively hide any eye-sores beyond, and they define the extent of the garden space.

An important point to remember is not to build walls too high, because this can create a feeling of claustrophobia. This problem has been successfully overcome by the introduction of an ornamental archway, with a wrought-iron gate. Besides alleviating any feelings of being 'hemmed in', the gate lures you to investigate interesting vistas beyond and makes the garden seem larger.

Hedges, although not as effective as masonry in reducing noise, do provide an alternative way of preserving the privacy of a garden, especially if they are evergreen, dense and tall. Closely planted firethorn (*Pyracantha*), cherry laurel (*Prunus laurocerasus*), or yew (*Taxus baccata*) make good surrounds.

Plants and masonry

An economical option that successfully breaks up the monotony of a brick wall is to leave gaps within the brickwork for planting. You can also decorate the top of the wall with plants.

Another choice, which has been used here, is to add a trellis above the wall. This acts as a decorative screen and can be covered within a year or two by rampant climbers such as *Clematis armandii*, ornamental grape-vine (*Vitis coignetiae*), Boston ivy (*Parthenocissus* species), hederas or the white-flowered climbing hydrangea (*Hydrangea petiolaris*).

Vertical gardening

A newly erected brick wall can, at first, appear rather harsh. It is a good idea to use climbing plants to blur this effect. There is an abun-

▼ **Background trees** Mature trees, in the garden and beyond, define the boundaries and enclose this private garden in a tapestry of green and golden colours.

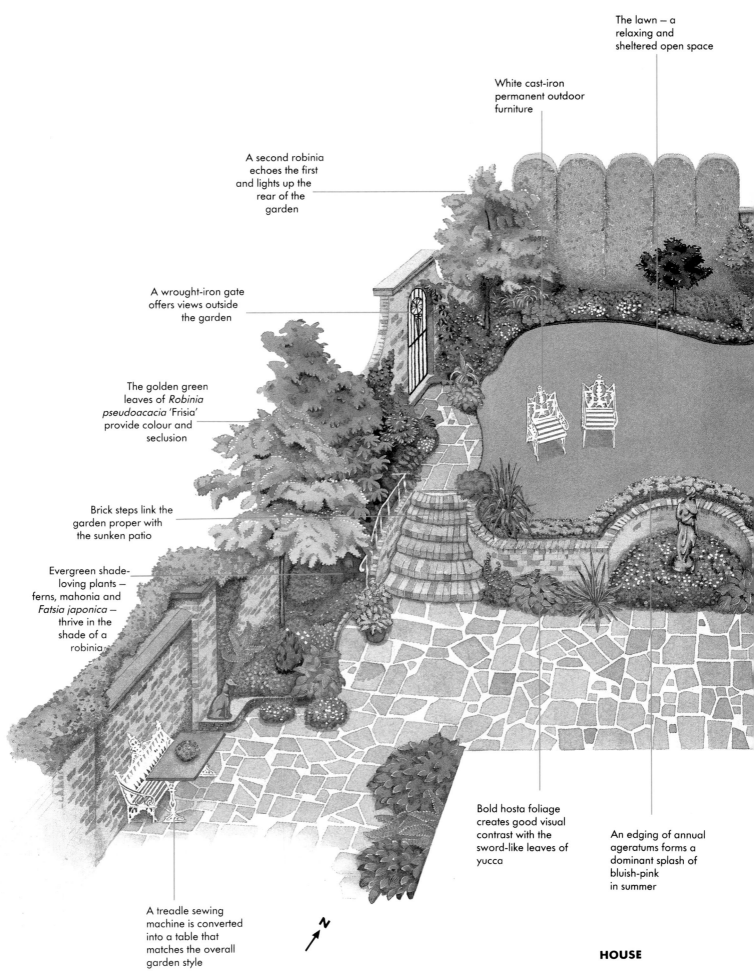

The lawn — a relaxing and sheltered open space

White cast-iron permanent outdoor furniture

A second robinia echoes the first and lights up the rear of the garden

A wrought-iron gate offers views outside the garden

The golden green leaves of *Robinia pseudoacacia* 'Frisia' provide colour and seclusion

Brick steps link the garden proper with the sunken patio

Evergreen shade-loving plants — ferns, mahonia and *Fatsia japonica* — thrive in the shade of a robinia

A treadle sewing machine is converted into a table that matches the overall garden style

Bold hosta foliage creates good visual contrast with the sword-like leaves of yucca

An edging of annual ageratums forms a dominant splash of bluish-pink in summer

HOUSE

Annuals like these marigolds are planted in definite swathes to avoid a cluttered look

Turreted brick walls form a decorative corner feature

A *Paulownia tomentosa*, with its distinctive heart-shaped leaves, is sited away from the house where its large size can be appreciated

Large-leaved *Vitis coignetiae* contrasts pleasingly with the small leaves of ivy 'Goldheart'

A columnar juniper adds architectural interest and winter greenery

Crazy paving covers the patio area in a well laid out pattern

dance of flowering climbers and a variety of ivies that will readily and rapidly grow up walls facing in any direction and enhance the whole garden.

Common ivy (*Hedera helix*) grows so abundantly that the newness of any brick wall can be obliterated within a year. Do bear in mind, though, that a few gaps in the covering are more appealing than a solid green mattress hugging the wall. The lush foliage setting of this garden is achieved by contrasting hues of green – for example, the light-coloured leaves of the golden acacia (*Robinia pseudoacacia* 'Frisia'), set against the darker ivy-clad perimeter walls of the garden.

Patio and steps

The crazy paving on the patio area is laid in a pattern of large and small paving slabs bedded in cement. It extends across the width of the site, with access from the house through French windows. It is on a lower level than the garden itself but linked to this with a flight of brick-built steps whose curving line is echoed in the abutting low wall.

The patio is a place for relaxing and large enough for informal entertaining, planting being contained within brick-edged beds, pots and containers and the odd

pockets along the base of the low walls. Sheltered on all sides, it receives afternoon and evening sun.

The steps are comfortably shallow and wide and lead, via a crazy-paving path, to an imaginary gate thus helping to create an illusion of space.

The furniture is a positive feature in its own right, and is part of the overall master design. The wrought-iron table and bench is matched by the slender banister alongside the steps and ornate chairs on the lawn. They are all painted white for maximum impact. The subtle and rather ornamental wrought-iron gate, fitted into the brickwork archway, completes the theme.

In a small, well-planned garden, weatherproof outdoor furniture is an advantage, though it does need regular maintenance to look its best. Collapsible tables and chairs need storage space, usually in a garden shed, which may not fit into the overall scheme. Also, furniture can brighten up the patio area, giving it an inviting feel, even in the winter months.

Plants in pots and urns provide

▼ **Shelter and seclusion** Safe from prying eyes and disturbing traffic noises, this little oasis looks across bright bedding plants and a velvety lawn to a soothing forest of foliage.

◄ **Peaceful greens** The patio is surrounded by foliage plants carefully chosen for their contrasts in colour and form — the huge hand-shaped and leathery leaves of *Fatsia japonica* beneath the finely divided, golden-green leaf sprays of false acacia. (*Robinia pseudoacacia* 'Frisia') right, and opposite, the spiky, white-edged sword fans of pot-grown yucca near blue-green hosta foliage and bright green arching fern fronds.

Pots and baskets of wax begonias punctuate the greenery with bright splashes of summer colour.

▼ **Garden statues** Inanimate objects can be difficult to site successfully, but the statue within the brick arch that marks the boundary of the patio looks perfect in the setting of hard surfaces with bedding and foliage plants. A semi-circle of ageratums weaves a garland that links the wall to the lawn.

an additional planting level which punctuates and accentuates the overall design. They add splashes of colour, toned down by the positive outlines, interesting shapes and foliage colours of the hostas and yuccas that add shape and form to the garden.

Lawn centrepiece

The two main features in this garden, shut off from the outside world with its brick walls and its mature trees, are the patio and the lawn. From the patio, the lawn appears larger than it actually is, partly because of its uncluttered appearance and partly because of its curving lines that flow imperceptibly into mixed borders and garden boundaries.

The lawn is perfect for sunbathing, with no chance of being overlooked. It has a soothing and rest-

ful effect, wonderful in the evening when the trees and shrubs cast their lengthening shadows. Its smooth expanse holds together the wide borders filled with shrubs, herbaceous perennials and colourful bedding plants.

Such lawn excellence is achieved only through loving care. Frequent mowing and edging, regular feeding and watering are the essential and, unfortunately, monotonous tasks that a gardener must be prepared to undertake in the pursuit of a perfect lawn.

Focal points

Throughout the garden are hidden little secrets, important for their particular impact yet blending naturally into the design. Statues are strategically placed among the

◄ **Shade lovers** In dappled shade for part of the day, the raised beds by the patio are filled with plants that thrive in just such conditions. Ferns and the tall, handsome leafy stems of Solomon's seal (*Polygonatum × hybridum*) arch over a footing of half-hardy busy Lizzies, the colourful carpet broken by a small-leaved trailing ivy.

▼ **Wall ornaments** The far corner of the garden, so often neglected, is a design feature of restrained elegance. The brick wall is pierced with a small niche containing a stone bust, and further along it is decorated with Victorian tiles, set flush in the walls like windows, and terracotta plaques. The crowning touch is a huge urn containing a handsome specimen of the male fern (*Dryopteris filix-mas*). It contrasts well with the bold foliage of the nearby foxglove tree (*Paulownia tomentosa*).

greenery – an inscrutable greyhound gazing across the patio, a Victorian bust in a wall niche, a graceful figurine rising like Aphrodite from a sea of busy Lizzies – and reflect the owners' personal style and taste. Such statues lend substance to clumps of shade-loving ferns and hostas and break up the solidity of walls; a single terracotta urn placed in the far corner draws the eye from the patio along a diagonal line that visually distorts and extends the distance.

A garden for dreams

Peaceful and secluded, the privacy of this garden has been achieved, at some cost, through a combination of clever design and architecture and through bold planting ideas. Like any other mature garden, it has been years in the making and the years to come will mellow the harshness of the surrounding walls and crazy paving.

The garden is by no means labour-saving – bedding plants must be renewed according to the changing seasons, climbers must be pruned to keep them within bounds and pot plants and containers need regular watering and feeding throughout the growing season.

The end result, though, is a green and restful sanctuary, a place in which to dream the dream of all gardeners – the creation of the perfect garden.

COURTYARD GARDENS

**Tiny urban gardens are often enclosed by
high walls and neighbouring trees. A creative design
can turn these into positive features.**

Town gardens are notorious for several things – shade, poor, dry soil, lack of privacy and lack of space – everything in fact to discourage gardening. Luckily, you can create privacy and an illusion of light, and improve the soil. What's more, in a small space you can justify the use of more costly materials and plants, and meticulous hard-landscaping details have greater impact than they would in a large garden.

Shade from buildings is unalterable, but shade from existing trees can be lessened by thinning out the branches. Check with the Local Council first; many trees are protected by law. Cutting down large trees (if permitted) may benefit the immediate gardens, but it does harm the landscape as a whole – and the oxygen level. Pollarding instead of tree-felling can often be effective.

Painting walls white can help to give the illusion of brightness and space, and pale foliage and pastel flowers have the same effect.

Improving town soil

The soil found in urban gardens is often drained of nutrients, resulting in disappointing plant growth. It can be improved by working in bulky organic matter. Sterilized compost or manure sold in bags by garden centres is useful.

Topsoil can be bought in bulk, but is expensive, and quality

▼ **False perspective** This long and narrow courtyard garden has been given an air of space and depth by an avenue of terracotta pots leading the eye along and up towards a group of slender Italianate cypresses at the garden boundary.

varies. An annual mulch of dried manure or forest bark chippings improves moisture retention and is a good soil conditioner. Regular feeds with quick-acting fertilizer provide ongoing nutrients.

Good-quality, loam-based potting compost gives containerized plants a head start, and there are special ericaceous composts for camellias, rhododendrons and other lime-hating plants.

Creating privacy
Old brick walls can look beautiful and new ones will mellow fairly quickly, giving a cosy enclosed feeling – but bricks and labour are very expensive. Thin 'walls' of trellis or interwoven fence panels can create privacy more cheaply.

An advantage of trellis is that, covered with deciduous climbers, it lets in the maximum amount of light during winter, yet filters light in summer, when a garden is used most. Deciduous standard-trained trees, with crowns above head height, also work well seasonally and are space-saving.

Town planting
Plant growth in urban conditions can often be slow. Large plants have instant impact, and though obviously they are more expen-

sive, can prove to be a sensible investment. However, they take longer to become established than small ones and need lots of water.

Planting closer together than normal, or over-planting, is also justified in a town garden, and again requires extra feeding and watering. Be prepared to discard some of the plants later on.

Town gardens are often too shady for a good lawn – or too small to make grass-cutting worthwhile. Choose a form of attractive paving instead.

A good proportion of evergreens gives small gardens an interesting aspect all year round.

◄ **Foliage dressing**
Glowing red brick laid in a
traditional basketweave
pattern makes an excellent
contrast for the dark green
wall coverings of Virginia
creeper and ornamental
vines. At ground level, brick-
red pots of clipped box echo
the colour scheme.

► **Centrepoint** A circular
pool surmounted by an
ornamental bird bath
introduces a different
geometric shape to
counteract the straight lines
elsewhere in the garden. A
wreath of small-leaved ivy,
that responds well to
clipping, surrounds the base
of the pool which is guarded
by two ornamental cranes,
poised to catch the goldfish
in the pool.

▼ **Flights of fancy** Wide
brick steps lead from the
house to the garden, marked
with bold terracotta finials
set on plinths. A low, densely
clipped box hedge and
standard-trained gardenias
repeat the architectural
design of the courtyard
garden below.

FORMAL BRICK

'L'-shaped back gardens are a common feature in many towns. In this sophisticated example, the long, narrow leg of the 'L' has become a plant-filled corridor; and the broad, square base near the house has been made into a calm, peaceful retreat.

Restraint is the dominant theme: the colour scheme is based on variations of brick-red, terracotta and dark green, and though some plants flower, they do so incidentally.

The layout is largely symmetrical – the few exceptions occur as a result of the garden's basic shape, or of whim. The stately steps, with their mirror-image ball finials, clipped hedges and topiary trees, align with the long corridor.

The fountain is central to the square, but asymmetrical when viewed from the house, making a pleasing break from static formality. And a seating area with a low wooden table is tucked into a corner that affords both shelter and privacy from onlookers behind the glass doors.

Hard landscaping

Restricting the number of materials used creates a feeling of space in a small garden. Surfaces appear to flow into one another, so disguising the real dimensions. Here, close-butted brick paving and low walls repeat the brick theme of the house and existing garden walls.

The brick paving is laid in a traditional, unobtrusive basket-weave pattern. On a practical level, using small units such as brick – as opposed to large flagstones – means that the paving can cope with uneven foundations and possible subsidence without ugly cracking. Such a design can incorporate manhole covers, gullies and drains with minimal visual disturbance.

Bricks – on the flat for risers and on edge for treads – form the steps that connect the small, upper entrance-way to the lower level of the garden. Brick edging to the beds reinforces the geometry, and on a practical note prevents soil spilling on to the paving.

Formal planting

Restraint and architectural form prevail, with dark green topiary, and dark green climbers taking the shapes of the walls they cover. Box is clipped into right-angled hedges, repeating the lines of the house and layout; and into topiary balls, echoing the shape of the finials. The round base of the fountain is surrounded by an immaculate ivy ring and filled with water lilies.

In the corridor is a 'forest' of clipped box balls, shortest in front and tallest behind. This gives an impression of depth and space to the corridor, as does a group of tall, Italianate cypresses at the far end of the 'leg'.

Temporary summer features, which must be housed frost-free during the winter months, include huge pots of cycas, or sago palms

(*Cycas revoluta*), maiden-hair fern and standard-trained gardenias. The palms, with their concentric rosettes, and the ferns, with their arching, fountain-like fronds, heighten the air of formality. The clipped gardenias repeat the shape of the topiary box balls. In contrast, a terracotta half-pot is filled with sprawling mint, containerized to prevent its roots spreading rapidly throughout the garden and sending up masses of suckers.

A mixture of climbers covers the walls: Virginia creeper, trumpet creeper, ornamental grape, Boston ivy, common ivy and Chinese jasmine (*Trachelospermum jasmi-*

noides). All are self-clinging. The Chinese jasmine has a summer display of scented white flowers, followed by the scarlet trumpets of *Campsis radicans*. The deciduous Virginia creeper (*Parthenocissus quinquefolia*) bears a modest amount of blue-black berries and the leaves turn orange and scarlet.

Features and focal points

The central feature is a two-tier round stone basin, with a pine-apple fountain head and goldfish in the pool. A pair of antique-style Chinese cranes watch over the fish, figuratively and literally, discouraging real birds from poaching them.

► **Soothing touches** The steps in this small urban garden have been given a new look with treads of concrete slabs. They will mellow with time, and meanwhile their bright appearance is softened with an evergreen mahonia, colourful tulips and a flowering crab apple tree.

BASEMENT GARDENS

Given an attractive layout and suitable plants, a small basement garden can be turned into a stunningly beautiful area and a restful retreat.

Though definitely challenging, even the smallest and most depressing basement garden can be transformed into a leafy retreat. Keys to success are imaginative design, improving the soil and choosing plants that are tolerant of shade and town pollution.

There are advantages to consider as well, such as the warm, sheltered environment often created by surrounding houses and garden walls. And because basement gardens are usually small, top-quality hard landscaping materials, such as paving, walling and trellis, are easier to afford than when dealing with huge gardens.

The site
The garden, of a Victorian terraced house, is rectangular, with a long, narrow extension 1.2m (4ft) below the main area, creating an 'L' shape. It is surrounded by a high brick wall which has been

made even taller by the addition of trellis at the top.

The garden plan makes the most of the feeling of space and luxuriant greenery, while achieving privacy by excluding unpleasant views as well as screening the neighbours' views into the garden.

This is a high-maintenance garden, which is attractive in every season. There is a continuous floral display from mid spring until the first autumn frosts.

The design
To provide privacy and help camouflage the small size of the garden, the boundary walls have been raised, then hidden with dense planting. The extra height gives additional space for vertical gardening, and increases the number of climbers and wall shrubs that can be grown, either in raised beds at the base of the walls, or in pots.

To create an element of surprise

and a feeling of extended space, a central feature divides the garden into smaller interlinked spaces. The pivot of the layout is an ornamental pool with a tall stone fountain. It is surrounded by multi-level planting beds. A statue provides a second focal point.

The pool and adjacent flower beds are set out at 45° to the garden boundary, and the surrounding paths are also on the diagonal. This makes them proportionally longer than if they ran parallel to the boundaries, and gives a feeling of generous width. The diagonals are repeated in the raised beds on the upper level, with increased planting frontage as a result.

▼ **Focal points** A softly playing fountain and a neo-classical statue are the two features that unite the multi-level planting beds and low-lying patio. They also convey a sense of intimacy and seclusion behind foliage-covered walls.

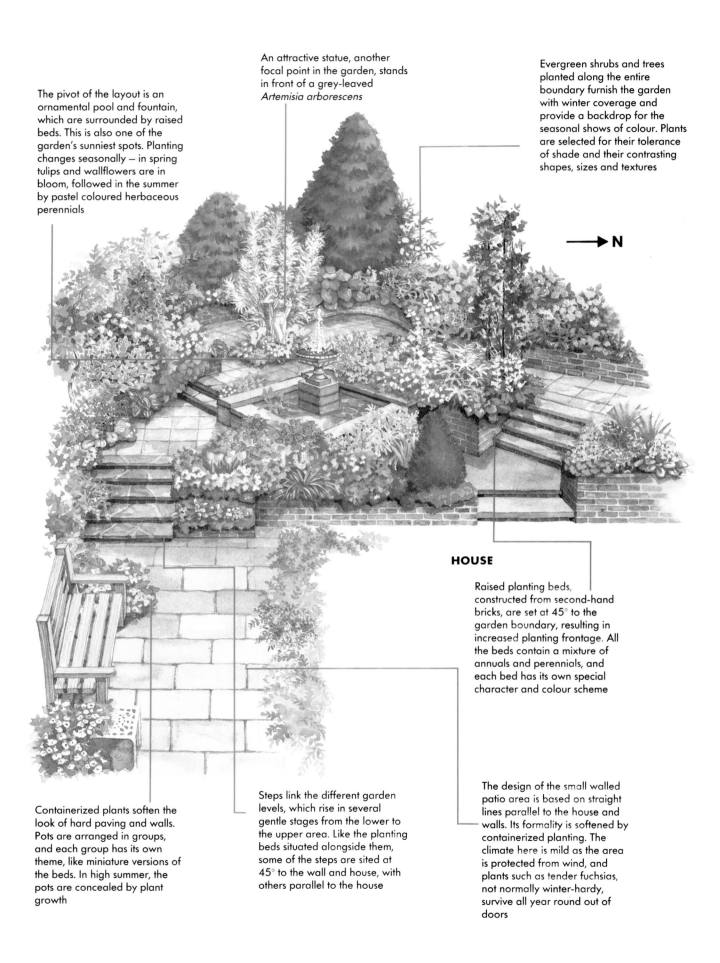

The pivot of the layout is an ornamental pool and fountain, which are surrounded by raised beds. This is also one of the garden's sunniest spots. Planting changes seasonally — in spring tulips and wallflowers are in bloom, followed in the summer by pastel coloured herbaceous perennials

An attractive statue, another focal point in the garden, stands in front of a grey-leaved *Artemisia arborescens*

Evergreen shrubs and trees planted along the entire boundary furnish the garden with winter coverage and provide a backdrop for the seasonal shows of colour. Plants are selected for their tolerance of shade and their contrasting shapes, sizes and textures

N

HOUSE

Raised planting beds, constructed from second-hand bricks, are set at 45° to the garden boundary, resulting in increased planting frontage. All the beds contain a mixture of annuals and perennials, and each bed has its own special character and colour scheme

Containerized plants soften the look of hard paving and walls. Pots are arranged in groups, and each group has its own theme, like miniature versions of the beds. In high summer, the pots are concealed by plant growth

Steps link the different garden levels, which rise in several gentle stages from the lower to the upper area. Like the planting beds situated alongside them, some of the steps are sited at 45° to the wall and house, with others parallel to the house

The design of the small walled patio area is based on straight lines parallel to the house and walls. Its formality is softened by containerized planting. The climate here is mild as the area is protected from wind, and plants such as tender fuchsias, not normally winter-hardy, survive all year round out of doors

▲ Bird's eye view Seen from the first floor balcony, the garden in miniature is a feast of greenery and floral colour, its regular contours well concealed.

Walking through the garden, a series of constantly changing views are presented, as sharp corners are turned and the same small space is seen two or three times from slightly different viewpoints.

The garden is made more interesting by several levels that rise in gentle stages from the lower to the upper area. Short, shallow flights of steps connect mini-landings.

The layout of the lower area, a patio, is based on straight lines, parallel to the house and boundary walls, and in strong contrast to plant forms. In the upper garden, the raised beds are laid out in two generous curves, springing from the diagonals, and these curves are reflected in the oval shape of the island bed. Curves give this area a separate character from the lower patio. They help conceal the straight boundary walls and provide planting areas of varying depths.

Construction materials
Careful planning has gone into the design of the garden. Locally obtained second-hand bricks are used for the step risers and the retaining walls of the raised beds. The step treads are built of existing York stone, plus bought-in reconstituted York stone pavings. The latter are also used to pave the patio and upper area.

To raise the boundary walls, 15cm (6in) holes have been drilled vertically along the top, at 1.2m (4ft) intervals, and steel rods, 1cm (½in) in diameter and 1.3m (4½ft) long, inserted. Strong wire mesh netting, 1.2m (4ft) wide, is attached to the rods, to create a barrier for cats. To conceal the netting, provide further privacy and an attractive support for climbers, white-painted wooden trellis panels are fixed to the rods. Garden and house walls are painted white, to reflect light and create an illusion of space and to provide a crisp, fresh backdrop for foliage and flowers.

Liberal amounts of bone-meal, dry cow manure and proprietary soil conditioner were dug into the soil before any planting took place. Mulches and slow-acting fertilizers are applied as a top dressing annually in spring.

Planting
Bright floral displays are set against a soothing background of greenery, provided by permanent shrubs, conifers and deciduous and evergreen climbers.

The beds are generally a mixture of permanent and temporary planting, but each bed has its own special character and a dominant colour scheme, with minor cross references to nearby beds. Because pale colours are more visible at night than deep ones, the main palette includes white, yellow, pink and pale mauve. It is not inflexible, though, and a few red roses, for example, are grown for their sweet scent.

Evergreen shrubs and climbers are used abundantly, to furnish the garden, provide winter coverage and make a setting for flowers. Various ivies, fatsia, and a hybrid between the two, × *Fatshedera lizei*, adorn the walls. There is a wide range of different leaf shapes, sizes and textures, and a balance between variegated and plain-leaved forms to add interest, but not frenzy. Ever-grey shrubs include *Senecio* 'Sunshine', lavender and the filigree-like *Artemisia arborescens*, planted round the base of the statue.

Plants are also selected for their tolerance of shade and less-than-perfect soil drainage. There are micro-climatic variations within the garden, though, and the sunniest beds are given to roses, underplanted with tulips, primu-

▲ Micro-climate The small paved patio, enclosed by white-painted walls and scented climbers, is sheltered at all times of year from the extremes of weather. Trailing fuchsias and busy Lizzies add colour to the greenery.

las and forget-me-nots in spring, and lime-green dwarf tobacco plants (*Nicotiana*) and green and bronze-leaved wax begonias in summer.

The second sunniest bed, a 1.2 × 1.8m (4 × 6ft) rectangular area by the pool, is a scaled-down herbaceous border. It contains phlox, campanula and achillea, and an area for summer bedding. In spring, the entire bed is filled with yellow wallflowers and white lily-flowered tulips. In early summer

there are yellow and white antirrhinums, pale blue petunias and an edging of pink begonias.

In the shady, north-facing raised bed, in front of climbers and shrubs, wallflowers thrive in spring, and in summer it is filled with bedding plants such as tuberous-rooted begonias, tradescantia and leaf begonias that put on a magnificent display for several months. On the shady patio, pots of dwarf bamboos, daphne, evergreen euonymus, fatsia and ivies thrive, together with cheerful white busy Lizzies.

Variation in plant height is also taken into consideration. A mounded effect is achieved in the flat beds by placing tall plants towards the middle of island beds,

or at the back of borders along the wall. For high-level interest, in addition to the walls, there are two pergolas, one supporting wisteria, and the other, ivy-leaved geranium (*Pelargonium peltatum*). A balcony overlooking the patio is planted with hanging fuchsias which trail gracefully, and intermingle with branching ferns and climbing wall-trained roses.

There is also a balance between formality and informality: clipped box hedging near the pool contains a cheerful sprawl of hyacinths, tulips and polyanthus in spring, and busy Lizzies in summer.

Philadelphus, lemon-scented verbena and honeysuckle are grown for the strength of their scent. The heavily fragrant, pink-tinged *Jasminum polyanthum*, usually grown as a house plant, thrives in the mild climate of the walled basement garden. Similarly, hybrid fuchsias and ivy-leaved pelargoniums, usually too tender to overwinter outdoors, are quite happy all year round, and reach massive size.

There is no room for a lawn, but smooth mats of mind-your-own-business (*Helxine*) edge the small terraced beds rising immediately above the patio, and transform them into tiers of green velvet. A variegated form of mind-your-own-business neatly edges the island bed created at the base of the statue, and serves as a soft foreground for the colourful spring and summer bedding plants that fill the bed.

Containerized planting
The patio relies on containerized plants to soften the look of hard paving and walls. Pots of different sizes are grouped in tight clusters, and those at the back are raised on bricks to give extra height. In high summer, the pots are concealed by the plant growth.

Some pots are double planted, for example with early-flowering regale lilies and late-flowering speciosum lilies, to give a display which lasts from mid summer to early autumn.

Plant care
If such a succession of plants are to grow luxuriantly and beautifully in the crowded, unnatural environment of an urban garden, they must be given large amounts of food and water. The plants receive an annual dressing of bone-

▲ **Shade-lovers** Each planting bed has its separate theme, of permanent and temporary plants, with the emphasis on foliage colour, form and texture. Shade-loving plants include the impressive hostas, from palest to dark green, marbled or strongly edged with white. Wax begonias and busy Lizzies also thrive in shade, their pastel colours becoming luminous at night.

◄ **Pool formality** The small garden pool is of classic shape and in perfect proportions with the rest of the garden. Sited in a sunny part, it is the pivot of the design and together with the fountain it introduces an air of tranquillity. The adjacent bed is bright with pale-coloured tulips and scented wallflowers in spring and perennials and bedding plants in summer.

meal, plus an occasional feed of
hoof and horn fertilizer. Proprietary plant feed is applied in early
and mid summer, and the roses
are also fed twice a year, with a
proprietary rose feed. Foliar feeding is given in emergencies.

Regular and generous watering
is necessary, because raised beds
and containers dry out quickly,
and the house and garden walls
themselves create a rain shadow.

There is a great deal of repet-
itive seasonal gardening. Spring-
flowering bulbs and biennials are
planted in autumn, then removed
and replaced with annuals in late
spring. These are in turn dug up
and discarded in autumn, except
for tuberous-rooted begonias,
which are lifted, dried off and
stored over winter.

▶ **Summer highlights** The green-clad
high walls by the patio are studded in
summer with splashes of colour from
hanging baskets of trailing fuchsias.
They do well in shade and in a
sheltered environment survive most
winters in the open.

▼ **Spring colour** The diagonal layout
and multi-level design make the garden
look larger than it is, particularly in spring
when growth is in the early stages.

SMALL PAVED GARDENS

**A garden floor made from paving rather than
grass combines well with cleverly chosen planting
– and is virtually maintenance free.**

In small gardens (particularly in front gardens), paving can be the ideal way of linking a number of features. It gives an impression of continuity and also diverts the eye from the size of the site. The small garden described here manages to convey a sense of intimacy and privacy, yet does not feel enclosed. This is partly due to its strong architectural framework, partly to the strong and clever design, and partly to the undeniable inspiration of a true plantsman who has brought the whole composition to vibrant life.

The framework
The owner started with very little apart from a basic rectangular framework of walls and buildings, enclosing an area of approximately 200 sq m/yd. The main house sits squarely at one end of the plot; opposite this, no more than 10m (33ft) away and on a slightly lower level, lies an old stable block that has been sensitively converted into guest accommodation. Stone walls form the remaining boundaries of the garden.

The ground drops a little to one side of the guest house, to form a small, secluded area.

Paving and steps
Hard landscape elements such as paving are the 'bones' or main structure of any garden design. In a small garden, simplicity is all-important – many a garden has been ruined by the introduction of too many conflicting patterns and surfaces. It is possible to be spoilt for choice – paving comes in so many colours, textures and sizes of natural and simulated stone that the floor of the 'outside room' can quickly lose its simplicity and end up as a jumble.

Paving materials should be chosen to reflect and harmonize with the surrounding buildings. With a brick house, for example, a brick paved patio will provide a good visual link between house and garden. Similarly, a courtyard adjoining a farmhouse could appropriately be paved with stone flags or granite setts.

▼ **Miniature lawn** Mind-your-own-business (*Helxine*) makes an unusual substitute for grass in a shady and damp area. However, it is invasive and needs frequent trimming to shape.

A small secret garden fits neatly into the slight change of level at the side of the guest rooms. This small space is itself divided into two. Next to the building lies a tiny sunken courtyard, paved with setts and furnished with pots and ornaments. Beyond the sunken courtyard is a delightful little water feature, set in a niche in the stone wall

N ←

Curving, gently meandering paths encourage dawdling and close scrutiny of the surrounding plants. They are allowed to encroach on the paths, with hardly any hindrance, heightening the general feeling of informality and subtly blending the hard and soft landscaping elements

A secluded paved sitting area in the centre of the garden is wrapped around with a soft semi-circle of foliage planting, which provides both shelter and privacy. The entrance to the central sitting area is narrow, like a doorway. This leads the eye forward, and from the opposite side directs attention back to the main house

HOUSE

An old stable block has been converted into separate guest accommodation. The main house sits squarely at the other end of the plot, not more than 10m (33ft) away. Stone walls form the garden's remaining boundaries

▲ **Granite floor** Setts laid in regular courses follow gentle curves. They are time-consuming to lay but once in place, they are maintenance-free and virtually indestructible.

In most modern-day situations, the choice may not be quite this obvious, but ideally no more than two materials should be used in any composition and they should complement the house.

This garden makes undemonstrative but subtle use of granite setts. They echo an element of stonework in the house and provide a mellow, uniform background.

The way in which paving, of whatever kind, is laid can make a considerable difference to the look of a garden. Here the granite setts have been laid in distinct courses, like brickwork. This produces strong parallel lines that lead the eye from side to side, opening the garden up and helping to create a feeling of greater space.

This effect is reinforced by steps running the full width of the garden and fronting the patio by the house. If these had been positioned differently, the overall sense of unity and spaciousness would have been considerably weakened.

In a walled garden, it is particularly important to create a feeling of spaciousness. Although walls

Granite setts are laid in distinct courses, like brickwork. This produces strong parallel lines that lead the eye from side to side, opening the garden up and helping to create a feeling of greater space.
Symmetrically laid, the granite setts seem to drift into the planting on either side

provide privacy and a useful support for climbing plants, they can also have a claustrophobic effect. Paths usually help to improve matters, giving a sense of movement and 'going places'.

A straight path encourages brisk walking, undesirable in a small plot. In this garden, the paths curve and meander gently, encouraging the walker to dawdle and observe the surrounding plants. Curves help to release a garden from its linear contours.

The two paths run either side of the garden, linking the buildings and giving a good view of the borders beneath the boundary walls. Cleverly laid, the granite setts seem to drift into the planting on either side, and plants are allowed to spill naturally on to the paths, unrestrained by staking. This heightens the general feeling of informality and subtly blends the hard landscaping elements with soft planting materials.

Planning for privacy

An open paved sitting area in the centre of the garden is wrapped around with a soft semi-circle of foliage planting, creating a feeling of seclusion.

While the central sitting area is the pivot and focus of the garden, there is also room for a secondary focal point, a small 'secret garden', which fits neatly into the slight change of level at the side of the guest rooms.

This small space, bounded by a stone wall on one side, has its own courtyard lined with granite setts and furnished with stone ornaments and plant pots.

Bright green mind-your-own-business (*Helxine*) occupies the centre of the courtyard and creeps along the dry-stone wall. Like the accompanying ferns and trailing ivy, *Helxine* thrives in shade, but can get out of control unless regularly trimmed to shape.

Beyond the sunken courtyard,

▲ **Stone baskets** Classic eighteenth-century stone ornaments, lavishly embellished with fruits and flowers, define the perimeters of the central sitting area. They are backed by clumps of feathery, bright pink cosmeas.

and hidden from the path by planting, is a delightful little water feature, set in a niche in the old stone wall. Although this is a natural mineral spring, a similar feature could be built in to any garden, fed by a submersible pump in a pool beneath.

This pretty feature is screened by foliage, so it remains invisible until the last moment – the perfect surprise at the end of the path.

Both these enclosed spaces or 'gardens within gardens' – the large central area and the small sunken courtyard – distract the eye from the strict rectangular boundaries and help to create a sense of spaciousness.

Planting schemes

While a strong basic structure and a well integrated layout are both essential to good garden design, it is the planting that brings the whole composition to life.

The choice of plants is very much a question of personal taste, but advance planning and restraint usually achieve more success than random planting. Most gardeners would want some background colour and interest throughout the year; they also aim to keep maintenance costs and effort down to reasonable levels. Shrubs and hardy perennials are less labour-intensive than annuals and bedding schemes.

Many people assume, quite wrongly, that the more plants you have, the harder it will be to keep things in order. In fact, the opposite is true, as a well-stocked garden and attractive ground cover allow weeds little room to develop.

In this garden the planting has been skilfully planned to provide interest across the seasons. The species have been carefully chosen, as much for foliage texture, colour and size as for flowers.

In late summer, the invaluable flowers of Japanese anemones (*Anemone japonica*), phlox, mallows and hydrangeas blend into a background of grasses, bamboos, hostas and the false castor-oil plant (*Fatsia japonica*).

Heights and shapes are cleverly juxtaposed – the dwarf, but clump-forming *Hebe rakaiensis* with its glossy green, narrow leaves and racemes of white summer flowers, contrasts with feathery silver artemisia and the quill-like leaves of fescues (*Festuca*), ornamental perennial grasses. The bold, sculptural leaves of *Hosta sieboldiana* or *Hosta albomarginata* make a perfect foil for ferns and the evergreen arrow bamboo (*Arundinaria japonica*).

Ideally, flower colours should harmonize with each other. Hot, strong colours – red, orange and mauve – demand instant attention and can overpower softer shades but they are useful in small groups to provide emphasis and contrast among foliage plants. The flowers in this garden are mainly in pastel shades, with pink, soft purple and white playing predominant roles.

Annuals – raised at home from seed or bought in from garden

▲ **Planting themes** The sitting area is enclosed by repeat planting on either side. Shrubs include mounds of hebe, blue-flowered *Ceanothus thyrsiflorus*, white *Hydrangea paniculata* and pink *Abelia* × *grandiflora*.

▼ **Shades of pink** Late summer brings a froth of pink, from shrubby *Lavatera olbia* 'Rosea' and the tall spikes of *Lythrum salicaria* 'Firecandle'. Later still, the pale green heads of *Sedum spectabile* turn russet-red.

centres – are useful for quick colour, for filling odd soil pockets and for providing cut flowers. They are indispensable while a garden takes shape and before the more permanent plantings fill out their allotted space.

Maintenance is always necessary, if only to prevent shrubs, hardy perennials and annuals from over-running each other. The temptation may be to let things grow as they will, without too much pruning, but a more ruthless approach must be adopted if you want to retain an attractive balance of flowers and foliage.

Many of the species planted here – including cotinus, viburnum, hydrangea and bamboo – would soon outgrow their allotted positions if not kept in check.

If a plant responds badly to persistent cutting back, or fails to thrive in a given position, dig it out and replace it with another species – or the gap might be filled temporarily with annuals.

Ornaments and furniture

Choose garden furniture and ornaments to tone in with surrounding planting and hard features. A lightweight table and chairs are just right in this particular garden. Ornamental stone baskets, filled with stone fruit and flowers, echo stonework elsewhere in the garden.

Solid granite spheres have good visual impact. In former times, such ornaments were placed on top of gateposts, supposedly to ward off bad luck.

In the final analysis, it is the sense of purpose and careful choice that make even the tiniest garden work well. Like here, everything should look right in its place and be perfectly in proportion to the space allotted.

Granite setts

Setts are cubes or brick-sized chunks of natural granite, once commonly used for street paving – they are increasingly difficult to obtain, but you might be able to buy them from a local demolition merchant, especially if you live in an urban area. Because of their small size, they are ideal for use in a free-form, informal design – they can easily be laid to follow a curve.

On the debit side, they are expensive, and need to be very carefully laid, to produce a perfectly flat and even surface.

▲ **Granite spheres** Perfect globes punctuate the lush planting of purple and variegated shrubs.

▼ **Cool retreat** Foliage plants of contrasting shapes, textures and colour furnish a quiet corner of the garden.

Designs for large gardens

Large gardens – in the town, country or suburbs – present a special challenge as well as offering endless possibilities. Without a carefully designed plan they can look like a series of compartments that bear little or no relation to each other. Site and position strongly influence the potential layout. In hilly, windswept situations, the necessary shelterbelts force the design to look inwards, while a garden with views over the sea, rolling countryside or a distant church spire can visually extend outwards beyond the actual boundaries.

The most successful designs for large gardens are simple and uncomplicated, with shapes relating to the geometry of the house and its surroundings. A ground plan may suggest patterns set square or at an angle or as a patchwork of circles. More complicated features, such as changes of level, raised beds and elaborate structures such as pergolas and formal pools, are easier to integrate where they seem to perform an obvious function.

Maintaining a large garden can be a challenge, but thoughtful planning and planting can cut the workload, by confining labour-intensive planting to the vicinity of the house and giving over the remaining garden to lawn and groupings of trees and shrubs.

Rural view Dry stone walling and hummocks of foliage plants blend naturally with the rural landscape.

FORMAL COUNTRY GARDENS

**Generally, gardens in the country are larger
and more labour-intensive than those in towns and suburbs.
A bold new design cuts maintenance to a minimum.**

In the angle of this cheerfully painted, L-shaped house is a dazzling courtyard area, ablaze with colour during the summer. It forms a wide stage from which uninterrupted views lead to large and tranquil lawns with island beds of sculptured conifers.

In a deliberate effort to enliven an already established garden, the immediate area around the house was redesigned as a large courtyard with numerous planting beds. The result is a separate flower garden, enclosed by low brick walls. Such strong demarcation lines work well only in large gardens. Because of the large expanse of lawns and established island beds, the transition from colourful intimacy to more formal layout appears wholly natural.

The courtyard area has been given a patchwork-like effect, with paved pathways running at right angles to the house, interspersed with broader areas paved with flagstones and alternating with gravel beds. The hard stone and grit, broken up by bright flower colour, make a good contrast to the soft, tranquil green background of lawns, bushes and trees. A low wall, built in brick to match the house, partly encloses the courtyard and marks the boundary between outdoor living room and garden proper.

Climbers and wall shrubs

The 'gingerbread' style house is enhanced with some fine planting of creepers and shrubs that part-cover the house and merge with the triangular gravel bed. Over the porch is a flowering honeysuckle, *Lonicera periclymenum*, and along the east-facing wall is an ornamental quince (*Chaenomeles speciosa*), its bright spring blossoms followed by small, edible golden yellow fruits.

A healthy specimen of Persian ivy (*Hedera colchica*) covers part of the south-facing wall of the house and trails down, past a fan-trained *Cotoneaster horizontalis*, rooting where it touches the ground until it is sandwiched between the rounded shapes of large lavender bushes.

The lavender truly prospers in this sunny corner and one or two have seeded themselves between gaps in the paving stones, and further away in the gravel beds. Another self-seeder is valerian (*Centranthus ruber*), both the red and white forms. It is a prolific plant for open, sunny situations and thrives in the poorest of soils.

Mats of purple campanulas and pale coloured rock roses overspill on to the paths and break up the

▼ **Planting beds** A patchwork of low-growing shrubs and perennials are criss-crossed by paving-slab paths and pockets of gravel. Hanging baskets and wall climbers provide vertical colour and interest.

gravelled areas. The pink flowers of thyme and the brilliant blue of speedwell (*Veronica teucrium*) give lively splashes of colour. The blues have the added attraction of 'picking up' and enhancing the deep blue of house doors and window frames.

Colour is also provided by a large number of pastel-shaded pelargoniums, some with variegated leaves, growing in square, round and columnar terracotta pots and hanging baskets.

More structure to the slightly raised paved area is given by garden ornaments – a large stone mushroom by the house, and a sundial by the far end of the path. A huge tree stump houses pots of ivy-leaved and fancy-leaved zonal pelargoniums and busy Lizzies. It effortlessly guides the view from ground level to the vertical expanse of climbers.

The triangular brick insets in

▶ **Change of pace** Shallow brick steps mark the level changes and the transition between paving and gravel surfaces. They echo the colour of the house and the low walls that enclose the courtyard area.

▼ **Colour harmony** Pinks and blues, to match the mellow red-brick of the house and the blue-painted woodwork, are the predominant colours in the summer season.

Paving slabs, gravel beds and low brick walls divide a brilliantly colourful display of small flowering shrubs, perennials and pot plants from the mature garden beyond. Decorative pots, a sundial, a staddle stone and a planted tree stump give additional interest. The house walls are clothed with ivies and honeysuckle, and hanging baskets overflow with summer colour

A golden yew — clipped square — forms the focal point in a large bed of mixed conifers and shrubs. The conifers display great variety of texture, form and colour, set off by a narrow edging of red begonias. The strong contrast between this bed and the flower planting near the house is most effective

N

A rustic pergola arches over a path of paving slabs and carries the eye away from the intimate planting near the house and out into other parts of the garden. The brick supports for the pergola echo both the brick of the house and the low brick walls surrounding the courtyard

An oblong bed contains mixed shrubs and perennials and provides a continuation of colour from the main flower planting into the green expanse of lawn

A second conifer and a bed of mixed shrubs complement the adjacent island bed. Both beds make for easy maintenance and provide a restful contrast to the colourful courtyard and the house

▲ **Island beds** Golden yew, clipped square at the top, and startling against dark green conifers, becomes an arresting focal point away from the courtyard's kaleidoscope of colours.

▼ **Welcome gestures** Hanging baskets, sweetly scented honeysuckle, twining clematis and clumps of lavender adorn the entrance and soften the hard surfaces of paving, brick and flint.

the paved area, together with the bricks confining the flower beds, subtly link this whole area with the brick of the house – small features but worth the investment of time and thought because they bring unity to this garden area and make it a coherent whole.

The whole paved area is demarcated from the rest of the garden by low red brick 'turreted' walls, bounding the paths on either side. Despite the lack of height – there are no raised beds or significant changes of level in this area – there is a feeling of intimacy closely associated with the house. The south-facing brick wall encloses a narrow sheltered border planted with thrift (*Armeria maritima*), aubrieta and hollyhocks, giving a distinctly 'cottage garden' atmosphere to this sunny corner.

The courtyard area curves out in the centre between the low brick walls, to a border of rounded shrubs which form an edging to the lawn. Among them are two excellent robust ground-cover shrubs – the vigorous, low-growing, scarlet-berried *Cotoneaster dammeri*, and the more rounded evergreen *Viburnum tinus*, with pink-budded white flowers in late winter and early spring, followed by clusters of blue to black berries in the autumn.

Conifer islands

A spectacular effect has been created in this garden by two large conifer beds and by individual specimen plants set into the lawn. There is a sculptural effect to the arrangement of one bed with its 3m (10ft) high, square-clipped golden yew (*Taxus baccata* 'Aurea') that contrasts strikingly with the dark green yellow-tipped foliage of a western red cedar (*Thuja plicata*) and a yellow-flowered potentilla. The whole bed – brilliant in its contrasting foliage colours, shapes and leaf textures – is set off by an edging of bright red bedding begonias.

There is an especially good view of this bed from the east side of the house. With lupins and poppies in the foreground, the view reaches ahead beyond the sundial with the large conifer bed to one side, and to the other side another conifer bed and a well-clipped mature beech hedge. Other planting in the lawn includes a spruce (*Picea abies*), and a triangular framework of stout rustic poles set into a small circular bed. A yellow rose ('Climbing Allgold') clambers up this framework, partnered by a large-flowered clematis 'Dr. Ruppel' (deep pink with carmine bars and golden stamens).

The island beds of conifers and shrubs provide a permanent framework that remains much the same all year round – they are green islands of rest and tranquillity which offset the busy, changing colours of the courtyard

▲ **Pillar rose** A rustic framework supports an attractive combination of climbers – the yellow rose 'Climbing Allgold' and the large-flowered, pink-red clematis 'Dr Ruppel'. Both respond to hard pruning in late winter.

◄ **Colour break** The large island bed of golden and dark green conifers appears all the more impressive as it rises from a footing of bright red wax begonias.

flower beds. The bold, formal shape of the square-clipped yew – immediately eye-catching – gives zest to the foliage planting. Yew is ideal for moulding into large architectural shapes but it is very slow-growing and it takes time to become bulky enough to cut to the desired outline.

The evergreens make for low maintenance – all they need is trimming to maintain the desired shape and size – while the lawn, with its broad, sweeping curves, is easy to mow regularly. The beech hedge needs one annual trim, in mid to late summer. It retains attractive brown leaves through winter. Maintenance is vitally important in a large garden and here all the labour-intensive gardening is concentrated in the flower beds near the house.

▶ **Plant container** A hollowed-out tree stump, replete with moss-covered edges, holds pot-grown zonal and ivy-leaved pelargoniums. It brings welcome height to an otherwise low planting scheme.

▼ **Evergreen cover** Persian ivy (*Hedera colchica*) clothes a house wall in green and gold; it trails around window frames and among *Cotoneaster horizontalis* before reaching the ground.

MODERN COUNTRY GARDENS

House style will always influence garden design, and the surrounding landscape can offer challenges as well as opportunities.

For many gardeners the challenge of creating privacy in a suburban or urban environment is of overriding importance. In open countryside the problem is reversed, and gardeners will seek to open up views to the rural landscape. The garden described here achieves a balance between the stark geometry of a modern country house and the surrounding hilly landscape. In addition, the proximity of the sea and the threat to plantings from salt-laden sprays made it necessary to create barriers against the prevailing winds.

The site
The landscape is windswept, hilly heathland, and the new garden and house lie in an isolated spot,

among fields. The garden is basically level and covers approximately 2500 sq m (3000 sq yd).

Mature trees nearby form a leafy backdrop and provide vertical interest and grandness of scale. The soil is free-draining.

The layout
The owners wanted an attractive, well laid-out garden, with a wide range of planting, and were prepared to maintain it well. The garden had to be attractive as well as tough, so that young children could use it freely.

The layout is simple – an expanse of lawn, with ornamental beds and borders around the house and hugging the garden boundaries. Beds and borders close to the house are rigidly geometric and

largely right-angled, to reflect the stark lines of the house itself; those further away are more sweeping and informal in plan, reflecting the transition from cultivated garden to an agricultural and wild landscape.

There is a sheltered, south-facing patio next to the house; from here are extensive views over the garden and the surrounding countryside. York stone paving connects the patio and various entrances to the house. It is laid in straight but zigzag lines to reflect the style of the house and to create

▼ **Rural aspect** On the sheltered side, low informal planting backed by rustic paling allows uninterrupted views from house and patio across rolling fields and woodland.

▲ **Ground cover** A large planting bed on the patio is filled with foliage plants, including ornamental grasses such as white-striped gardener's garters (*Phalaris arundinacea* 'Picta') and low clumps of blue fescue (*Festuca glauca*). Thyme creeps among cracks in the paving, and above it all stands a splendid tree of heaven.

→ **N**

The boundary on the sheltered southern side is merely marked with post and rail fencing and low-growing perennials so as not to impede the wide views over rolling fields and woodland

Tough, wind-resistant maritime pines (*Pinus pinaster*) are planted as specimen trees in the lawn, to filter the wind and provide year-round interest. These pines thrive in sandy soil

Closely mown lawn spreads a green carpet around house and borders. It sets off flower colours and leaf forms and contrasts with the fields beyond

Shelter belts of cotoneaster, elaeagnus and olearia protect the northern, eastern and western boundaries from salt-laden sea sprays. They are themselves shielded by a wind barrier of mature trees outside the garden

York stone paving surrounds the house. Laid in a geometric pattern that complements the architecture of the house, it receives sun for most of the day. The large surface is broken up by several planting beds and softened with creeping plants and sprawling foliage

The patio faces due south and is sheltered by the house. It is ideal as an outdoor living room in summer and enjoys extensive views across the garden to the rural surroundings

planting beds. The paving is flush with the lawn, to facilitate mowing.

Salt-laden winds are a potential threat to planting, so the northern, eastern and western boundaries are planted with tough screening plants. The southern boundary, which is sheltered and overlooks cornfields and an apple orchard, is demarcated with low post and rail fencing in keeping with the agricultural aspect. Clumps of native perennials – achilleas, ox-eye daisies and campanulas – frame the view.

Planting design

Plants are the major feature, and a wide range of planting enlivens the simple layout. It is not a connoisseur's garden, and most of the plants are popular, ordinary and easily available.

The selection is pleasingly varied: trees, shrubs and perennials; old-fashioned, cottage-garden plants including pinks (*Dianthus*), Jacob's ladder (*Polemonium*) and yellow loosestrife (*Lysimachia*); sea-side plants, brilliantly coloured under the sharp light and offset by subtle

▲ **Architectural flair** Plant silhouettes break the rigid angles of the house. A silver birch rustles above green laurel bushes and yellow-flowered rose of Sharon (*Hypericum calycinum*).

foliage odours. The main criteria are toughness, character and a contribution to the overall 'texture' of the garden.

In all successful planting designs, all plants are positioned so as to gain the maximum contrast of form, foliage and colour. Foliage is as important as flowers, and this garden contains a wonderful mix-

ture of foliage: spiky, lacy, rounded, glossy, furry, variegated and many shades of green.

Ornamental grasses such as miscanthus, blue fescue and green-and-white striped gardener's garters are a feature, along with variegated ground elder, a sophisticated cultivar of the dreaded and invasive weed. Flower colours come from roses, poppies, alstroemerias, day lilies and Michaelmas daisies, and in late winter and spring from naturalized bulbs.

Near the patio and paving, low-growing plants are tightly grouped in dense clumps, mounds and carpets of ground cover. Here and there, they are encouraged to spill on to the paving, softening the right-angled geometry of the layout. Tiny creepers make their way along cracks between paving slabs, which are laid without grouting.

There is a rough gradation in

▲ **Seaside gardens** Maritime pines are ubiquitous to mild coastal areas. At maturity, they bear shiny brown cones that stay on the trees for years.

▼ **Harvest fields** In late summer, spikes of yellow loosestrife and clumps of Michaelmas daisies merge into the fields of ripening corn.

heights, from low at the plant boundaries to high around the house. Trees provide most of the high-level interest.

A young, multi-stemmed ailanthus rises out of a large planting bed on the patio. *Ailanthus altissima*, or tree of heaven, is a deciduous, very hardy and fast-growing tree, usually seen as a single-stemmed specimen tree. If cut back, as here, it forms a graceful, multi-stemmed tree with ash-like leaves as much as 1m (3½ft) long. Female trees have long bunches of yellow-red, 'key'-like fruits in summer.

When fully mature, the ailanthus will become the pivotal point of the whole garden; the house may even seem to have been planned around it. A multi-stemmed cut-leaved sumach makes another strong focal point in an island bed on the north side of the house.

The lawn is neatly mown. It has been left uncluttered in the centre, to increase the sense of space, with specimen conifers sited near the borders that follow the contours of the garden.

The colour scheme

Green is the predominant colour, and provides a cool framework for vivid splashes of bright yellow, purple, red and blue. Even slightly garish colours – that of the floribunda rose 'Orange Sensation' for example – fit in well.

Colour is used in bold groups and drifts among the background green rather than being dotted around at random. By the patio, pastel shades predominate while the stronger colours are reserved for the boundary borders.

Coastal climate

The winter climate is comparatively warm in this area, so slightly tender plants, such as eucalyptus, olearia (the white-flowered daisy bush that revels in coastal climates), New Zealand flax (*Phormium*), New Zealand burr, and the yellow-flowered *Pittosporum tobira*, with its heavy orange scent, are planted as permanent features outdoors. (In cooler regions, these can be grown in large containers and moved to frost-free sites for the winter.)

Even the cabbage palm (*Cordyline australis*), planted as a lawn specimen near the patio, will survive most winters here.

▲ **Windbreaks** Tough evergreen shrubs of cotoneaster, elaeagnus and olearia create a dense barrier to filter salt-laden winds from the sea. As shelterbelts, evergreen plants are more effective than walls or fences.

◄ **Colour points** The bright blooms of 'Orange Sensation' rose are subtly toned down by the dark green leaf fans of New Zealand flax (*Phormium tenax*).

Maritime pines and junipers are part of the natural vegetation of the area; both the species and their more sophisticated cultivars are used in the planting. Pines are set out as small specimen trees on the lawn, singly and in groups; they will fill out with the years.

Dwarf pines in the flower beds and borders provide year-round colour, especially important when the herbaceous plants are dormant. Junipers, both upright and horizontal, contribute further evergreen interest to the borders.

What is omitted from this modern garden is as important as what is included. There are no bedding schemes or short-lived plants needing frequent replacement. There are no statues, pools or fountains, flower pots, urns, balustrading or railings. The house and garden plants speak for themselves.

SUBURBAN GARDENS

**In restricted spaces, a garden design
based on plants with strong visual impact
throughout the year is all-important.**

The word 'suburban' in garden descriptions can sometimes sound dismissive. In fact, a well laid out suburban garden can be as beautiful, in its own way, as any grander scheme.

With its rectangular plot ending at the pavement and a side drive leading to the garage, this garden contains the typical components of a suburban garden: boundary hedges, a lawn, and beds with evergreen and deciduous shrubs, bulbs and perennials.

What sets this garden apart from the ordinary is the rich variety of plants. The owners are avid plant collectors – there are all sorts of surprises in the planting, which give the garden a memorable character. Another special quality is the use of space: not a single inch is wasted, yet no plant is uncomfortably crowded.

The layout

The garden, measuring 21 × 10.5m (70 × 35ft), faces north but the plot is not overshadowed. It has an open, airy feeling with only the area immediately outside the house in shade. The site slopes gently away from the house, and is sheltered by boundary hedges and a neighbouring house. The soil is free-draining, acid sand. The mature boundary hedges of mixed conifers, weigela, laurel and privet are kept pruned well back to give the most space.

The owners enjoy growing plants from seeds and cuttings and wanted to display their vast collection without giving any feeling of a formal botanical garden. This informal scheme, with an S-shaped lawn, sets off the plants well.

Between the lawn and driveway a narrow island bed was created

for conifers. A path leading from the drive to the front door divides the peat garden in front of the house from the mixed border opposite. Finally, a semi-wild mixed border was established along the front boundary.

The peat garden

The owners like ericaceous plants, and a peat garden has transformed the shady corner by the house into a positive asset. The ground was excavated to a depth of 30cm (1ft) and lined with perforated black polythene sheeting

▼ **Suburban garden** A traditional layout includes lawn, paths, beds, mixed borders and specimen trees. However, it is the choice of plant materials that lifts a garden from the commonplace to the unique through the changing seasons.

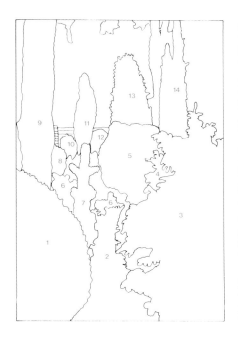

CONIFER BED

A wide variety of conifers, from pencil-slim to bun-shaped and from soft gold to blue-grey, bring visual interest throughout all seasons of the year as well as extending a degree of privacy to the garden. The plan identifies some of the main conifers in the collection.

1 Golden dwarf thuja (*Thuja occidentalis* 'Rheingold')
2 Columbine (*Aquilegia vulgaris*)
3 Spruce (*Picea abies* 'Acrocona')
4 False cypress (*Chamaecyparis lawsoniana* 'Lanei')
5 Sawara cypress (*Chamaecyparis pisifera* dwarf variety)
6 Dwarf noble fir (*Abies procera* 'Glauca Prostrata')
7 Pine (*Pinus aristata*)
8 Japanese cedar (*Cryptomeria japonica* 'Spiralis')
9 Irish juniper (*Juniperus communis* 'Hibernica')
10 False cypress (*Chamaecyparis lawsoniana* 'Ellwood's Gold')
11 Golden Irish yew (*Taxus baccata* 'Fastigiata Aureomarginata')
12 Dwarf Sawara cypress (*Chamaecyparis pisifera* 'Squarrosa Sulphurea')
13 Golden thuja (*Thuja occidentalis* 'Lutea')
14 Pencil juniper (*Juniperus scopulorum* 'Skyrocket')

to conserve moisture. The excavated soil was mixed with peat substitute, leaf mould and gravel. A 30cm (1ft) high wall was built round the bed, and the soil mixture returned to the excavation to form a raised peat garden.

Typical North American, Asiatic and European acid-loving species are grown here. The main season of display is spring, but there is some colour during the rest of the year; snowdrops in winter, for example, and brilliant blue autumn-flowering gentians.

Masses of dwarf rhododendrons fill the peat garden with colour from mid spring to early summer, together with pieris and dwarf shrubs such as the slender-stemmed bog rosemary (*Andromeda polifolia*) and bilberries.

There are no true heathers, but the related mountain heaths (*Phyllodoce*) carpet the soil with their narrow, dark green leaves and bell-like flowers.

The moist, cool, acid soil and shade are ideal for herbaceous and bulbous woodland plants such as dog's-tooth violet (*Erythronium*) and wake robin (*Trillium*). Wood anemones, purple-leaved violets and the hardy cyclamens enjoy the same conditions. There are also several terrestrial orchids, including pink lady's slipper, and clumps of deciduous ferns.

Single and double-flowered sanguinarias are grown for their ruffled leaves and waxy white spring flowers. Their common name, bloodroot, comes from the red sap the plants exude when cut. Pale blue hepaticas, resembling the anemones to which they are related, provide spring colour at the same time as snowdrops.

An unusual feature of the peat bed is *Arisaema triphyllum*, a North American arum-like plant. Its strange white-veined, purple-brown spathes appear in early summer.

The conifer bed
The owners wanted as wide a range of conifers as possible. Because of limited space they chose selected examples of each type: pencil- or bun-shaped, horizontal-growing or dwarf, in a range of contrasting colours.

Many were grown from cuttings or transplanted from friends' gardens; others were bought or traded at the local garden society.

Spacing trees and shrubs is always a compromise, since allowing for the ultimate spread can leave a garden looking bare for years. Here, the owners decided to space the conifers according to medium-term rather than long-term growth. A few conifers, potentially too big for the garden, were included for their unique appeal.

After a couple of decades, the conifer bed is pleasantly full, but a great deal of discreet pruning is needed during the growing season. Where pruning is ineffective, or could disfigure the conifer, the plant is carefully lifted and root-

◀ **Raised peat garden** Cool and moist, acid soil is essential for the rhododendrons that burst into glorious bloom in late spring. It also suits heaths and heathers, dog's-tooth violets and woodland plants like trilliums and wood anemones.

▲ **Slimline conifers** Slender junipers and Irish yews retain their narrowly columnar shape well into maturity, with a minimum of pruning. They add vertical interest to small beds, and the golden forms create focal points.

◄ **Leaf contrasts** The large, spear-shaped leaves of *Arum italicum* 'Pictum', marbled grey and green, are in stark contrast to the near-yellow foliage of *Hosta fortunei* 'Albopicta'. In the background, the feathery leaves of peonies keep a modest presence.

► **Open-plan garden** In spite of dense planting, the garden feels open and airy, due to its lack of obvious boundaries. An annual mulch of pulverized forest bark keeps the soil cool and weed-free.

balled in autumn and passed on to friends. This gives the roots time to become established before the cold weather sets in.

Shearing back growth of fast-growing conifers, such as columnar *Cupressus macrocarpa* 'Gold-crest', keeps them compact and dense; in the case of this particular conifer it also encourages production of the rich golden, feathery juvenile foliage.

It is also a good idea to pinch out the growing tips of slow-growing

conifers during the growing season. Though time consuming, this
bonsai-like practice results in
dense branching and compact but
exaggerated form.

Slender, pencil-shaped conifers
are a special feature of the garden.
Juniperus communis 'Hibernica'
and *Juniperus scopulorum* 'Skyrocket' are favourites and retain
their slim shape naturally.

Border plants

The mixed border is dominated by
a golden honey locust (*Gleditsia
triacanthos* 'Sunburst') which
starts the season with a bright,
golden glow. The border also contains a yellow-flowered tree peony
(*Paeonia lutea* var. *ludlowii*),
Elaeagnus × ebbingei, and variegated pittosporum. The shrubs are
underplanted with clumps of
hostas, poppies and day lilies.

The semi-wild garden refers not
so much to the type of plants but to
the owners' relaxed attitude
towards the dry bed near the road.
Here, bulbs multiply undisturbed
– they include crocus, especially *C.
tommasinianus*, *Allium trique-
trum*, colchicums, daffodils and
tulips. Mat-forming silver artemisias and the golden form of creeping Jenny (*Lysimachia nummularia* 'Aurea') provide later cover.

There are masses of rudbeckias
and Michaelmas daisies for late
summer colour. Shrubs include
the Venetian smoke tree (*Cotinus
coggygria*) and yellow-leaved
Berberis thunbergii 'Aurea'.

▲ **Ordered wilderness**
Bulbs in the border are left to
multiply and come up year
after year. Pink and white
tulips and clumps of white-
flowered ornamental onions
(*Allium triquetum*) poke
through a golden ground
cover of creeping Jenny
(*Lysimachia nummularia*
'Aurea').

◄ **Good companions**
Thoughtful planning results in
fine associations of
complementary forms and
colours. Central to this group
is a clump of spiky blue oat
grass (*Helictotrichon
sempervirens*) partnered by
a creamy-yellow peony and,
on the right, the bright
foliage of *Spiraea japonica*
'Goldflame'. On the left is a
golden dwarf conifer
Chamaecyparis pisifera
'Filifera Aurea'.

ELIMINATING EYE-SORES

**Large, dominant structures can be difficult
to disguise but with imaginative design and careful planting
they can become attractive features.**

All too often people treat their gardens simply as a single-level enclosed space containing unrelated features – whereas a unified three-dimensional approach is often much more rewarding. This applies especially when dealing with a difficult, angular-shaped garden with large projecting structures. However, by using a range of design techniques and sympathetic planting, hard, obtrusive, vertical lines can be altered and intrusive structures disguised or incorporated into the overall layout.

This garden comprises an awkward, slightly wedge-shaped space with a garage in one corner and a conservatory in another.

Creating unity

The problem of large, dominant shapes within a flat, rectangular plot has been overcome by designing the garden on three distinct but linked levels, and by turning an intrusive garage into an attractive feature.

The garden's large central area is emphasized by the sweeping curves of a lawn which begins at the French windows and terminates in a shady pool of green at the far corner of the garden. The lines of the lawn swing the focus away from the garage and on to a large sycamore tree. The marked curvature of the lawn is further strengthened by a low brick wall that surrounds the semi-circular

sunken patio adjacent to the conservatory. The shape is repeated in a low rosemary hedge that flanks the curving path.

The flowing lines of the path – made of tinted concrete – unite the different sections of the plot and echo the curving projections of the garage in one corner and the conservatory at the other end of the diagonal.

The garden's second level is created by a series of raised brick-built beds which have been filled

▼ **Design disguise** The flat rectangular plot has lost its awkward shape through the introduction of curving lines and changes in the level of beds and patio.

with evergreen shrubs and trailers. The plants help to mask and soften the boundaries and large structures.

The third level consists of the sunken, brick-paved patio. A generous shallow space, three bricks lower than the lawn, it is perfect for entertaining and for viewing the rest of the garden.

Disguising an eye-sore

What could have been an ugly intrusion – the corner garage – has been transformed into an attractive feature. The garage is built from mellow brick and the building's most obvious feature – the long wall – directly faces the conservatory and patio. The garage could not be totally hidden but its outline has been effectively obscured and softened.

The garage walls, embellished with piers of brick, have been turned into a decorative feature with the addition of mock Gothic windows and an ornamental lion's head fountain and basin.

Water spouts from the lion's mouth to drop into a semi-circular, bricked-in water tank. The base of the tank is hidden by clumps of euphorbias and a small-leaved hebe, and flanked by a pair of spindle-shaped conifers. At night, the tank and lion's head are lit from below.

Vertical brick piers link the garage façade with the concrete posts that support the timber boundary fence. A single trim of red bricks laid horizontally along the top of the garage wall also helps to unite the timber with the trelliswork at the rear of the garden.

The red brick pattern is repeated at the base of the garage walls, where it both enlivens and is broken up by the rounded shapes of herbaceous plants.

Viewed from the garden, the dark Gothic-style windows contrast pleasantly with the unadorned lighter brickwork. The play of light and shadow around this hard feature is matched by the green variations in the planting scheme.

Conservatory and patio

The large circular conservatory balances the effect of the garage and acts as a link between house, patio and garden. Two mellow brick steps lead from the conservatory to the patio, which has a basketweave-pattern brick floor.

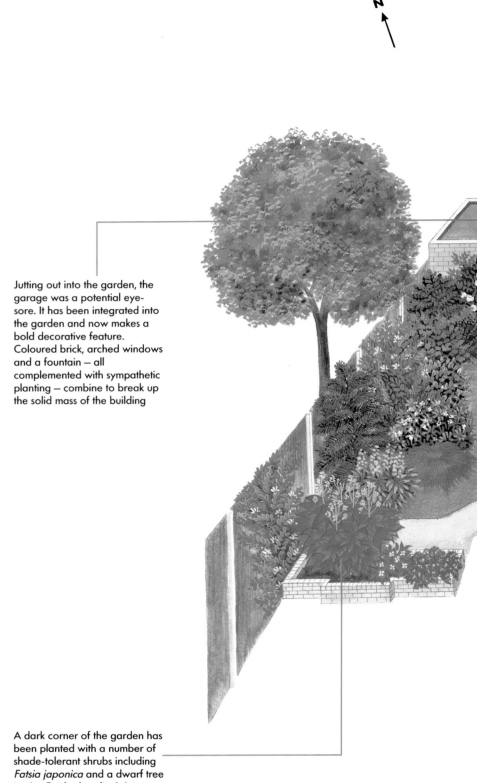

Jutting out into the garden, the garage was a potential eye-sore. It has been integrated into the garden and now makes a bold decorative feature. Coloured brick, arched windows and a fountain – all complemented with sympathetic planting – combine to break up the solid mass of the building

A dark corner of the garden has been planted with a number of shade-tolerant shrubs including *Fatsia japonica* and a dwarf tree ivy (× *Fatshedera lizei*). Lesser periwinkle (*Vinca minor*) gives good evergreen ground cover

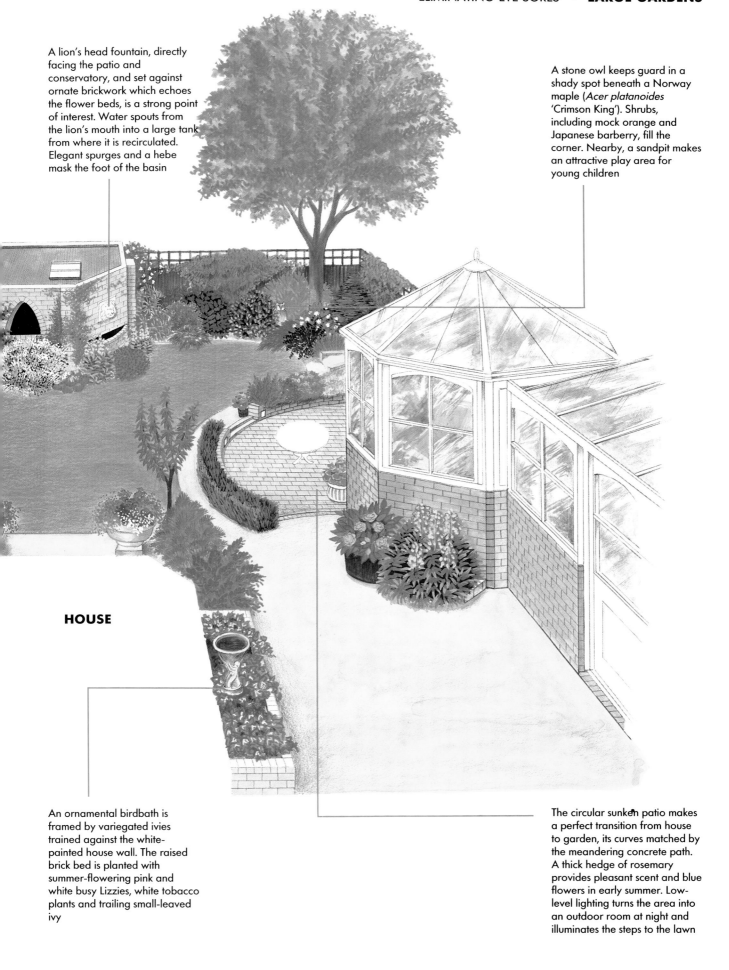

A lion's head fountain, directly facing the patio and conservatory, and set against ornate brickwork which echoes the flower beds, is a strong point of interest. Water spouts from the lion's mouth into a large tank from where it is recirculated. Elegant spurges and a hebe mask the foot of the basin

A stone owl keeps guard in a shady spot beneath a Norway maple (*Acer platanoides* 'Crimson King'). Shrubs, including mock orange and Japanese barberry, fill the corner. Nearby, a sandpit makes an attractive play area for young children

HOUSE

An ornamental birdbath is framed by variegated ivies trained against the white-painted house wall. The raised brick bed is planted with summer-flowering pink and white busy Lizzies, white tobacco plants and trailing small-leaved ivy

The circular sunken patio makes a perfect transition from house to garden, its curves matched by the meandering concrete path. A thick hedge of rosemary provides pleasant scent and blue flowers in early summer. Low-level lighting turns the area into an outdoor room at night and illuminates the steps to the lawn

99

The patio wall is broken by wide, shallow steps which lead up to the lawn – low-level lighting illuminates the steps and shows off the surrounding rosemary hedge at night. Facing west, the patio gets the best of the evening light. An unobtrusive stone and metal barbecue is recessed into the patio wall.

The low rosemary hedge provides a pleasant aromatic scent, and blue flowers in summer. Despite its low height, it is dense and compact enough to provide a degree of seclusion – without hiding the rest of the garden. Regular clipping keeps the hedge in shape.

On the other side of the steps, following the curve of the patio, is a raised bed containing mixed herbs that repeat the rosemary theme and link the patio to the adjoining flower bed. Here are shrub roses and a buddleia that partly conceal a small triangular, sunken sandpit.

▲ **Clever disguise** From being an obtrusive eye-sore, the massive garage wall has become a decorative feature. Embellished with coloured brickwork, wall-mounted fountain and Gothic-style windows, it now appears as an integral element in the garden design.

▼ **Boundary markers** A trellis-topped fence supports a sweet-scented honeysuckle and a repeat-flowering climbing rose. A glossy-leaved Mexican orange (*Choisya ternata*) and the silvery-grey foliage of *Senecio greyii* give evergreen camouflage to the wall.

Garden ornaments

Occasional stone ornaments, pots and urns dotted around the garden are filled with a variety of foliage plants, summer bedding and bulbs. A stone owl, well hidden in

the shadows cast by a mature Norway maple, has become mossy with age and provides a surprise element – flanked by the scented white blooms of *Philadelphus* and the prickly stems and purple-green leaves of *Berberis thunbergii* which colour richly in the autumn.

The interplay between light and shade can also be seen in the stone birdbath by the house. The base of the figurine nestles among a small-leaved variegated ivy, while the birdbath itself is framed by a backdrop of a larger darker leaved variegated ivy (*Hedera canariensis* 'Gloire de Marengo') which partly and luxuriantly covers the white wall. Colour contrast is provided by four blue and white tiles, decorated with flower and bird motifs, set higher on the wall.

Elsewhere in the garden – by the conservatory, on the patio and close to the house – are several terracotta and stone containers. A wooden half barrel contains an evergreen camellia.

The planting scheme

The garden is planted with a wide selection of easily maintained shrubs and shrubby perennials which form the backbone of the planting. The overall effect is one of a leafy perimeter consisting of plants with different colours and textures of foliage.

On the sheltered west side of the garden, the high wooden fence is partly covered with climbing hydrangea (*Hydrangea petiolaris*) and blue-flowered Californian lilac (*Ceanothus* sp.). The adjacent bed has, among other plants, red-leaved berberis, the dark green glossy leaves of sweetly scented Mexican orange (*Choisya ternata*), the light green leaves of flowering currant and a small-leaved cotoneaster. These shrubs create a multi-tiered, living covering which effectively disguises the tall fencing.

By the garage, in contrast, paler leaved shrubs, such as grey-leaved senecio, have been used to brighten the façade and modify the dominating effect of a large expanse of brickwork. Ultra-hardy white-flowered royal lilies (*Lilium regale*) and the white-flowered climbing summer jasmine (*Jasminum officinale*) provide colour. Exotic spurges, including *Euphorbia wulfenii* with its showy green-

▲ **Wall features** Architectural touches – coloured brickwork, Gothic-style arches and a lion's head fountain – turn a previously ugly feature into an attractive focal point. Evergreen planting at the foot of the wall and scrambling climbers above heighten the effect.

▶ **Brick buttresses** Large piers break up the garage wall, and climbing roses and summer jasmine add to the disguise. The raised planting bed at the foot contains majestic, white trumpet lilies and sprawling, woolly-leaved lamb's ear (*Stachys lanata*).

▼ **Play corner** A sunken sandpit is set in a quiet corner close to the patio. Summer colour comes from fragrant white-flowered mock orange (*Philadelphus*) and from an edging of garden pinks.

▲ **Ivy garland** Large-leaved variegated ivy (*Hedera canariensis* 'Gloire de Marengo') covers the white-painted house wall and frames an ornamental bird bath. In shade for much of the day, the raised bed is planted with busy Lizzies, white tobacco plants and small-leaved trailing ivy.

◄ **Culinary herbs** A simple barbecue is recessed in the boundary wall of the patio. It is conveniently surrounded by a bed of fragrant herbs. Pink-flowered ceanothus and evergreen, false castor-oil plant (*Fatsia japonica*) hide the wooden fence.

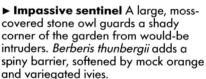

► **Impassive sentinel** A large, moss-covered stone owl guards a shady corner of the garden from would-be intruders. *Berberis thunbergii* adds a spiny barrier, softened by mock orange and variegated ivies.

yellow flower heads, are used for border contrast with darker leaved plants. The green-yellow theme is reinforced by common lady's mantle (*Alchemilla mollis*).

The garden has a strong spring planting scheme. Grape hyacinths (*Muscari tubergenianum*) and early hellebores (*H. corsicus* and *H. foetidus*) are grouped beneath the water fountain.

Tulips have been planted under climbing and shrub roses. Three varieties of tulips make bold splashes of colour – the single early, golden-orange 'General de Wet', the mid season carmine and white 'Garden Party' and the sal-mon-pink 'Clara Butt' which flowers in late spring.

Blue-flowered spring anemones (*Anemone blanda* 'Atropurpurea') are planted in a pair of urns either side of the French windows.

SHADED GARDENS

Large trees shut out light with their overhanging branches, but the problem is easily solved with shade-tolerant underplanting.

Dealing with a garden overshadowed by tall trees can be a daunting prospect but, if they are attractive enough and provide privacy, trees can become an essential part of the garden design. By choosing shade-tolerant plants, the problem of tree-shadow can often be solved.

Many plants, particularly shrubs, do well in varying degrees of shade. These are plants that naturally live in forest areas, or in the dappled light of woodland glades. Many tend to have modest flowers but colourful berries – some of which may last from late summer through the winter months. Many such shrubs do best on the slightly or markedly acid soil resulting from the build-up of rotted leaf litter.

The garden described here lies on slightly acid, moist soil. It has been improved over the years with garden compost and shredded forest bark. The garden has been stocked with a wide variety of shrubs, many of Asian origin, such as the spotted laurel (*Aucuba*).

The back of the house faces north-west, and the garden is L-shaped. Apart from the extensive shaded area, other points of interest include a water garden, an adjacent area planted as a rock scree, and an attractive pergola around which shrubs and climbers that appreciate full sun have been planted.

Coping with shade

The long arm of this L-shaped garden is cast in shade for much of the day by the overhanging branches of several large yew trees. The lower branches of some specimens have been lopped off but there is dense shade over a good half of the garden, including the lawn. The immaculate condition of the lawn is due in part to the high quality of the original turf, made up of a shade-tolerant lawn seed mixture with a high proportion of fine fescue grass (*Festuca*). The lawn is regularly fed throughout late spring and summer with liquid manure.

The lawn is the strong unifying feature. Its gently rippling form extends from one corner which lies in deep shade to the diagonally opposite, well-illuminated side. The undulating lawn is surrounded by scalloped and straight

▼ **Moist shade** Many plants thrive in shade, provided the soil beneath is moist. Here, spotted laurel, cotoneaster and fatsia make sizeable mounds beneath large mature yew trees.

borders planted with a good mix of flowering shrubs which help to disguise the straight lines of the perimeter walls and the stone flagging of the patio.

Plants for shade

In a bed at the foot of the garage wall and adjoining the patio, grow shrubs that do not object to the shade cast by the wall. The brightest spot is reserved for a golden-leaved form of the common box (*Buxus sempervirens* 'Aureo-variegata'). Its small leaves and slow growth contrast with a wall-grown vigorous *Pyracantha atlantioides*, decked in summer with billowing white flower clusters and in autumn with scarlet berries. The evergreen planting also includes a spring-flowering camellia which thrives in the moist, acid soil.

The east-facing border, backed by a brick wall, is dominated by massive yew trees that cast permanent shade in spite of the lower branches having been lopped off. The sweeping curves of the lawn have created deeply undulating planting beds in which the yews appear as integral parts of the design. In the deepest shade are planted evergreen shrubs that are tolerant of such inhospitable sites – spotted laurel (*Aucuba japonica*), which is easy to grow and not averse to air pollution, and the equally accommodating false castor-oil plant (*Fatsia japonica*) with its huge, glossy and deeply divided leaves.

Further along the border, shrubs are grouped to give a tiered effect, showing off differences in leaf form, colour and size. A low-growing cotoneaster (*Cotoneaster horizontalis*) is flanked by Japanese maple (*Acer japonicum*) and skimmia (*Skimmia japonica*). The cotoneaster produces small pink flowers, succeeded by clusters of scarlet berries. Skimmias have fragrant creamy flowers and, if male and female plants are grown together, small, bright red berries. Their glossy, leathery green leaves contrast with the soft green of the maple which turns deep red by late summer. Shade-tolerant red and white busy Lizzies edge the curve.

Further along is a Mexican orange (*Choisya*) which benefits from the sheltered position. It bears white flowers with a scent of orange blossom in late spring.

Mature yew trees shade much of the garden for most of the day. However, their lower branches have been lopped off to allow some light to filter through and shade-tolerant shrubs have been used extensively for underplanting. With their dark green foliage and red berries, the yews are attractive in their own right

Shade-tolerant shrubs, many producing flowers and berries, fill the strongly curving border. Spotted laurel (*Aucuba japonica*), false castor-oil plant (*Fatsia japonica*) and low-growing *Cotoneaster horizontalis* provide a mix of leaf colour, size and form

A circular pool is visible from every part of the garden and breaks up the curving sweep of the large lawn. Although in dappled shade from the trees, it catches the morning sun. A stone bench set against a backdrop of ornamental grasses and flowering shrubs makes a pleasant seating area. Water playing from a small fountain provides a soothing note

A scree bed, built on builders' rubble and topped with quartz chippings and rocks, is tucked behind the pool. Dwarf conifers and mat-forming alpine plants dominate the planting, with alpine pinks and gentians for colour accents

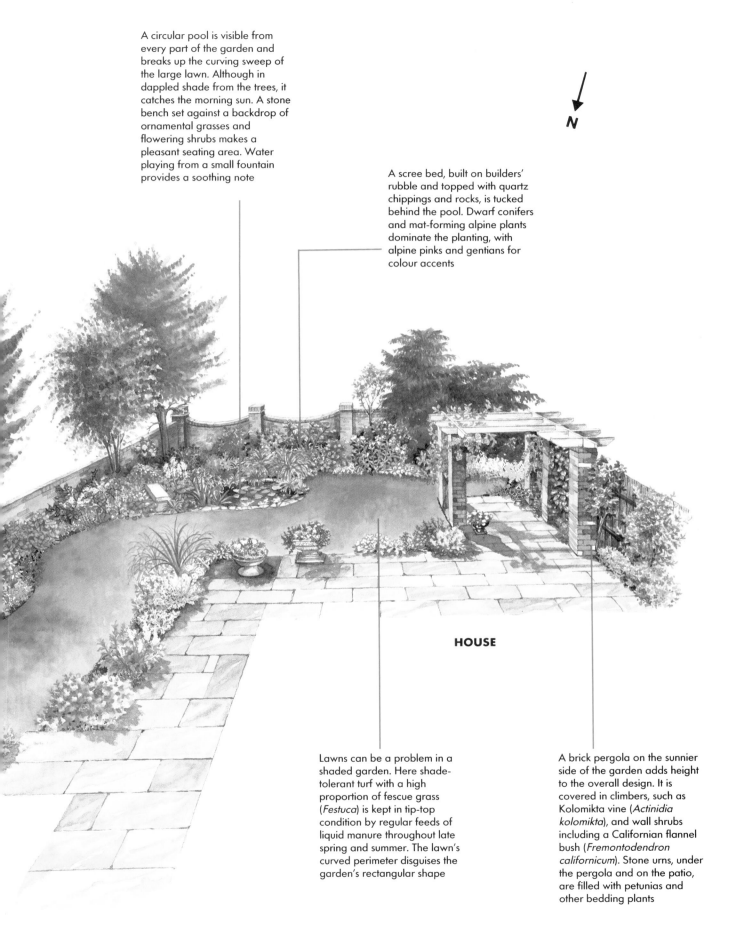

N

HOUSE

Lawns can be a problem in a shaded garden. Here shade-tolerant turf with a high proportion of fescue grass (*Festuca*) is kept in tip-top condition by regular feeds of liquid manure throughout late spring and summer. The lawn's curved perimeter disguises the garden's rectangular shape

A brick pergola on the sunnier side of the garden adds height to the overall design. It is covered in climbers, such as Kolomikta vine (*Actinidia kolomikta*), and wall shrubs including a Californian flannel bush (*Fremontodendron californicum*). Stone urns, under the pergola and on the patio, are filled with petunias and other bedding plants

▲ **Pergola walk** A brick-built pergola with an open timber roof adjoins the sunny and sheltered patio. It is furnished with half-hardy climbers, hanging baskets and urns planted with summer bedding.

▶ **Water and rock** A circular pool, stocked with water lilies and irises, is set in a wide sweep of the curving lawn. In dappled shade for most of the day, the pool and neighbouring scree bed draw the attention from house and patio. Waterside vegetation — hostas, cord grass and the creamy flower plumes of meadowsweet (*Filipendula ulmaria*) — create a feeling of semi-wilderness.

An interesting corner

The main sweep of the lawn leads to a small circular pool with a surround of random York stone. Plants such as wild strawberry (*Fragaria vesca*) spill over the wide paving.

The pool is sited in dappled shade, and the harmonious and varied planting around the feature makes it an especially pleasant, tranquil spot. Poolside planting includes clumps of hostas, tall erect spikes of water iris, feathery, plume-like flowers of meadowsweet (*Filipendula* sp.) and a cascade effect from the green

and white leaves of variegated cord grass (*Spartina pectinata* 'Aureo-marginata'). White water lilies and a white form of marsh marigold occupy the pool.

The pool is stocked with small koi carp and can be illuminated by a spotlight positioned below the water surface. A low fountain plays from a statue set into the centre of the pool.

Behind the pool, hardy shield ferns (*Polystichum setiferum*) screen a second feature – a miniature scree slope. It is slightly raised above the general level of the garden with builders' rubble

and hardcore taken from the site. This material has given the scree the free drainage necessary to accommodate a range of alpine meadow plants.

The rubble has been topped with grey and pink quartz chippings which give a light and colourful effect. For a 'natural' look, rocks of different shapes and sizes jut out from the scree.

The plants chosen for the scree area are tough and need minimum care. They are mainly mat-forming plants of different shapes and colours – golden moss (*Sagina glabra* 'Aurea'), New Zealand burr

(*Acaena* 'Blue Haze') and the spectacular saxifrage *Saxifraga* 'Tumbling Waters'. This forms a silvery rosette, rather like a spider's web, with strap-shaped leaves and a very large single white flower spike. Spots of colour on the scree come from alpine pinks, summer-flowering gentians (*Gentiana septemfida*) and clumps of fruiting alpine strawberries.

Dwarf conifers, of different shape and foliage, give height to the scree bed: golden-green, crowded and vertically held sprays of *Thuja orientalis* 'Aurea Nana' contrast with the greeny-blue soft foliage of *Chamaecyparis lawsoniana* 'Minima Glauca'. A clump of bamboo, its grassy leaves

arching above the wavy leaf rosettes of *Polygonum bistorta*, frames one side of the scree; at the back, a young Japanese maple (*Acer palmatum* 'Dissectum'), with finely cut green leaves, will turn gloriously red in autumn.

The sunny side

From the French windows of the house is a view across the wide paved area that forms the patio and the pergola walk. The paving is a mixture of real and simulated York flagstones. At the end of the garden is another group of mature yew trees fronted by shrubs and herbaceous perennials and framed by a substantial brick pergola.

The pergola supports consist of

► **Wall climbers** Warm red bricks, irregularly laid, form a pleasing background for such half-hardy shrubs as New Zealand pittosporum. Held in place at the pillar with wire, the colour of the pale green and creamy-white variegated leaves is picked up in a footing of white-flowered potentilla.

In a sheltered recess between pillar and fence, a kolomikta vine shows off its tri-coloured foliage.

▼ **Idyllic retreat** A peaceful corner bathed in morning sun, the small stone seat by the pool matches the surround of York stone paving. The small statue, half hidden among lush vegetation, conceals a softly playing water fountain.

PLANTS FOR SHADE

Aucuba japonica – evergreen shrub; white flowers; red berries.
Brunnera macrophylla 'Variegata' – perennial; green, white-splashed leaves; blue flowers.
Buxus sempervirens – evergreen shrub; green or variegated forms.
Convallaria majalis – perennial; rich green leaves; white flowers.
Digitalis grandiflora – perennial; green hairy leaves; creamy-yellow flowers marked brown.
Dryopteris dilatata – perennial fern; broad, arching fronds.
Euphorbia robbiae – evergreen sub-shrub; greenish-yellow flowers.
Fatsia japonica – evergreen shrub; green leaves; white flower clusters in autumn.
Gaultheria shallon – evergreen, suckering shrub; leathery green leaves; pinkish-white flowers; purple berries.
Hedera helix vars – evergreen; dark green/variegated leaves.
Helleborus corsicus – evergreen perennial; greyish leaves and yellowish-green flowers.
Hosta fortunei 'Aureo-marginata' – moisture-loving perennial; lilac flowers and yellow-green leaves.
Hypericum calycinum – evergreen ground cover shrub; bright green leaves; yellow flowers.
Hydrangea macrophylla – deciduous shrub; green leaves; pink, blue or white flowers.
Ilex aquifolium – evergreen holly; long, dark green leaves; red berries if female plants are pollinated.
Iris foetidissima – dark green, evergreen leaves; insignificant purple flowers; brilliant red seed pods.
Lamium maculatum 'Roseum' – evergreen perennial; nettle-like leaves; pink flowers.
Ligustrum japonicum – evergreen privet; glossy dark green leaves; white flowers.
Mahonia aquifolium – evergreen shrub; dark green leaves, red-purple in autumn; yellow flowers.
Saxifraga fortunei – perennial; green/purple-red leaves and white flowers.
Skimmia japonica – low evergreen shrub; white flowers and red berries if male and female plants grown.
Vinca major – evergreen sub-shrub; blue-mauve flowers.
Vinca minor – evergreen sub-shrub, often variegated; white, blue, red, purple flowers.
Viola cornuta 'Alba' – perennial ground-cover plant; heart-shaped leaves; white flowers.

London stock bricks to match the external walls. A spotlight fixed under the pergola roof is used at night to illuminate pale-flowered plants around and just beyond the pergola framework. The plants include the creamy-white, shrubby hydrangea (*Hydrangea arborescens* 'Grandiflora'), the white-variegated form of dogwood (*Cornus alba* 'Elegantissima') and, at ground level, the white periwinkle (*Vinca minor* 'Alba').

Because the pergola receives the full afternoon sun, some half-hardy shrubs and climbers do well in the sheltered recess formed between pillars and fence. The Californian flannel bush (*Fremontodendron californicum*) is a large-growing, semi-evergreen shrub with handsome three-lobed, rather fig-like leaves and stunning golden-yellow flowers throughout summer and autumn. Here also grows the kolomikta vine (*Actinidia kolomikta*), a slender climber outstanding for its leaf variegations of green, creamy-white and pink.

Twining around the pergola is sweet-scented winter jasmine and, for spring colour, *Clematis montana rubens*. A variegated *Pittosporum* grows up one pillar, merging with a pale-flowered potentilla at ground level.

A hanging basket filled with bright coloured ivy-leaved geraniums gives a splash of summer colour – a theme picked up by bold-coloured petunias planted in urns on the patio, and by the white and salmon-pink busy Lizzies at the front of flower beds.

Keeping existing trees
The question of what to do with existing mature trees is important when you are redesigning a garden. The temptation is to cut down large trees – provided they are not subject to a preservation order by the local council – to allow more light for other plants, but it is well worth thinking twice before doing this. Large trees bring an air of maturity to a newly designed garden and cannot be replaced in less than 15 to 20 years.

Rather than cut down a tree outright, consider careful lopping or pruning of some of the larger branches to bring the tree to a suitable size and shape.

The garden design here has incorporated the yew trees, whose dense shadows could have been a problem, and made them into an asset. Yews, in spite of being poisonous in all their parts, are attractive for their evergreen foliage and their sprays of bright red berries.

▲ **Woodland sites** Moist shady conditions are ideal for such foliage plants as hostas and many woodland ferns, including shield ferns (*Polystichum* sp.). They mark the transition between poolside and a moist scree bed.

▼ **Scree bed** Simulating an alpine meadow, a small moist scree garden appears as a natural extension of the pool surround. It is planted with mat-forming, creeping evergreens among the rocks and with ferns and dwarf conifers to add height and provide foliage contrast.

Design for a purpose

Like houses, gardens become expressions of a personality or lifestyle, and for this reason, priorities change with the years. Ideally, a garden should be planned to reflect the changing needs of the owners and have something to offer every member of the family. Children need space to play and areas to hide in, and most adults want a place in which to relax or entertain and beds in which to grow plants and vegetables.

For some people, practical functions are less important, so the garden design may focus more exclusively on plant content. With a well thought-out planting concept, it is not difficult to create a secluded garden where plants take priority and shape, colour and texture become the deciding factors.

Sometimes physical or time constraints dictate that low maintenance outweighs all other considerations. In such cases the immaculate lawn yields to trouble-free paving, and plants that look after themselves replace time-consuming herbaceous borders. Similarly, you can create visual deceits with images that are mere illusions but trick the eye and produce three dimensional effects, for example, a trellis that leads the eye to a non-existent vanishing point.

Play areas Family gardens, however small, should include spaces for children's activities.

GARDENS FOR CHILDREN

**A family garden should cater for the
wishes of all members, with space for youngsters to
play and adults to relax.**

Every parent knows the pleasure of being able to open the kitchen door and let out a boisterous child or children for a spell in the garden. Whether five minutes or a whole afternoon is spent playing outside, it gives the parent a break, and the youngsters a chance to exercise in the fresh air in a supervised environment.

On the other hand, very few parents are willing to give up all their rights in the garden. They are reluctant to allow it to become the outdoor equivalent of an untidy playroom, full of toys and half-completed children's projects, with nowhere peaceful or orderly for adults. Compromise is the best solution, and it can be most attractively done.

Design changes
Originally, this garden was a long, narrow, flat plot – well maintained but lacking in character. Composed mainly of lawn, the south-facing garden had a crazy paving path straight down the centre, cutting the garden into two narrow strips and leading to a wooden shed at the bottom, and bordered by narrow flower beds.

The layout was altered to meet the needs of a family with two small children: a low-maintenance garden based on an interesting design that incorporated large, simple shapes and different levels.

The new design includes a lawn and seating area, a children's bicycle track and a play area with a climbing frame. A terrace and outdoor dining area for entertaining, as well as privacy from neighbouring houses and gardens have also been achieved.

Although the garden is on the outskirts of a large town, the planting has a definite 'country' feel, rather than a sophisticated,

urban look. High priority is given to fruit trees, shrubs and perennials – useful for flower arranging – and plants for year-round cover.

Creating a new garden
Circles form the basic geometry of the new layout. A wide, curving path connects terrace, sunken dining area and lawn with the shed and play area at the rear.

A strong diagonal axis is created by siting the circular lawn and sunken dining area asymmetrically, so that the path has to curve first in one direction, then the other. This makes a first-class cycle track, as well as creating an illusion of additional width to the garden.

The space left between the circular shapes and the garden

► **Circular themes** Clearly defined areas separate spaces for relaxation and for play. Patio, sunken dining area and hard-wearing lawn are surrounded by a curved bicycle racing track that visually alters the narrow garden.

boundaries becomes low raised beds, the extra topsoil coming from the excavation of the dining area. The flower beds are 15cm (6in) higher than the main garden level, and the dining area is sunk to a depth of about 45cm (18in). Drainage here is provided by a gully at its base, which is linked to the main drains.

The play area is at the back of the garden and partly shielded by shrubs. Children can enjoy a feeling of secrecy, and the climbing frame, slide and rough ground don't detract from the general appearance of the rest of the garden. The ground beneath the play equipment is covered with coarse forest bark chippings, but ideally it would have a proprietary safety surface in order to minimize accidents. The curving path becomes a natural extension of the play area, and is as good for roller-skating as for cycling.

Privacy from the neighbouring houses is provided by sturdy trellis fixed to the top of the existing wooden fence along all the boundaries. Fruit trees, climbers and wall shrubs are trained against the fence.

Layout variations

The garden layout could equally well be based on more formal lines, with a generous-sized square or rectangular lawn and similarly shaped sunken dining area substituted for the circular ones in this garden.

In some ways, it would be an easier alternative. Laying bricks in circular or other curved patterns – especially tight curves to a small radius – can involve extra work in cutting bricks to shape or having to vary the width of the mortar between bricks.

For a children's garden, though, curves are ideal. The service path that doubles as a children's racing track would offer less scope if it went at right angles round square lawn and dining areas. A straight path could cause young children to slip at abrupt turns, or tempt them to cut corners, resulting in muddy patches at the edges of the lawn.

However, generous in-filling in such corners with brick paving laid at a 45° angle to the path would allow for fast, safe cycling and would also break up the straight geometric lines of a rectangular layout.

▲ **Adults only** A circular brick-built dining area adjoins patio and house to which it is connected with shallow steps. Covered with lush climbers, the boundary fence affords a degree of privacy, and from the surrounding raised bed wafts the scent of an evergreen rosemary hedge, covered in late spring with tiny blue flowers.

In a design based on circular shapes, the depth of the borders thus created varies widely. Such a device adds interest to the planting and also serves to disguise the proportions of the garden. An alternative layout based on rectangles would result in straight beds parallel with the path at the long boundaries and at right angles to it at the bottom and near the dining and patio area.

Future changes

The layout is designed to be flexible, and easy to adapt when children's amenities are no longer needed. A vegetable garden, with a row of flowers for cutting, might eventually replace the play area. The spot is convenient, being partially hidden from view and could also accommodate a small greenhouse.

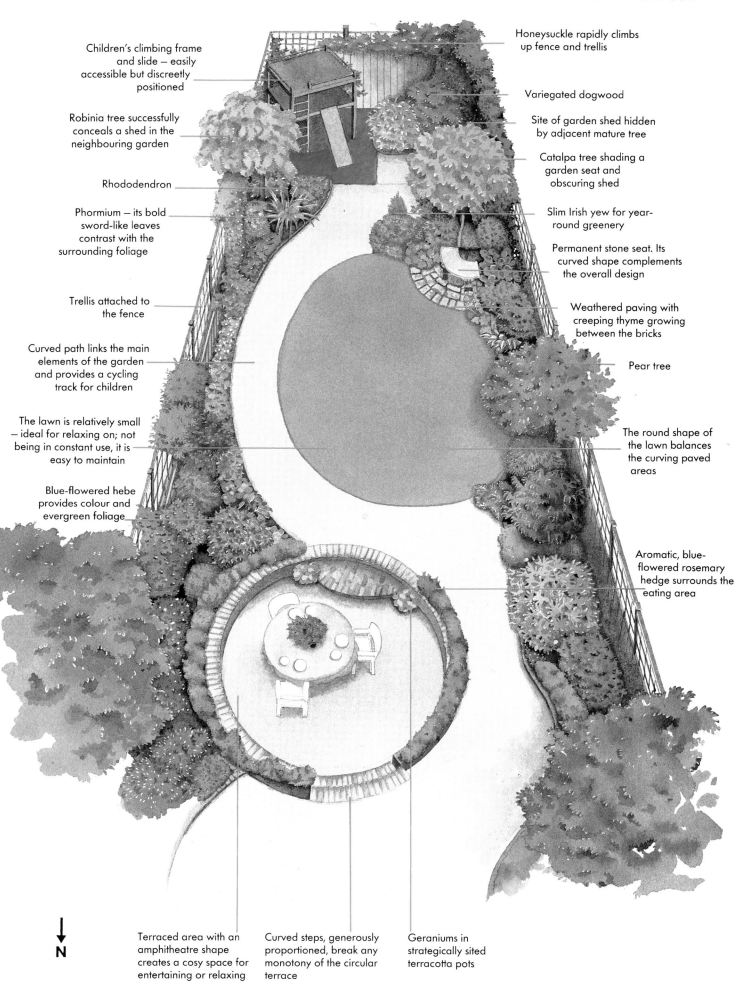

Children's climbing frame and slide – easily accessible but discreetly positioned

Robinia tree successfully conceals a shed in the neighbouring garden

Rhododendron

Phormium – its bold sword-like leaves contrast with the surrounding foliage

Trellis attached to the fence

Curved path links the main elements of the garden and provides a cycling track for children

The lawn is relatively small – ideal for relaxing on; not being in constant use, it is easy to maintain

Blue-flowered hebe provides colour and evergreen foliage

Honeysuckle rapidly climbs up fence and trellis

Variegated dogwood

Site of garden shed hidden by adjacent mature tree

Catalpa tree shading a garden seat and obscuring shed

Slim Irish yew for year-round greenery

Permanent stone seat. Its curved shape complements the overall design

Weathered paving with creeping thyme growing between the bricks

Pear tree

The round shape of the lawn balances the curving paved areas

Aromatic, blue-flowered rosemary hedge surrounds the eating area

N

Terraced area with an amphitheatre shape creates a cosy space for entertaining or relaxing

Curved steps, generously proportioned, break any monotony of the circular terrace

Geraniums in strategically sited terracotta pots

HOUSE

Although the rear part of the garden is slightly shaded by the end boundary fence, the area does get enough light for the normal range of flowers and vegetables. Some vegetables, for example lettuce, spinach and radishes, appreciate protection from fierce summer sun.

A small water feature could be incorporated in the design at a later stage. It is inadvisable to install even a small pool while toddlers are around, but later they will be fascinated by water and the wildlife it attracts – fish that dart about, birds that come to drink or chase insects and frogs that mate and spawn.

Once the children grow older, ornamental pots may be set out in groups along the path. Filled with fuchsias, geraniums or other bedding plants, they will add summer colour without causing accidents or being knocked over.

The boundaries

A timber fence is an ideal choice for the boundary. It can easily and effectively be hidden by climbers, trees and shrubs – a sense of intimacy is created by disguising the boundary in this way. A brick wall, on the other hand, is not only vastly expensive, but it also attracts the eye, drawing attention to the perimeters of the garden and emphasizing its small size and narrow shape.

Whatever material the boundary is made of, trellis makes a good finishing detail at the top, since it lets light and air in at the same time as providing privacy and support for plants.

The planting

As is often the case in urban gardens, the original acid soil was thin and lacking in nutrients. However, it was easily improved by the addition of coarse pulver-

ized bark and slow-acting organic fertilizer. Well-rotted manure would have worked equally well, but can smell overpowering in a small town garden.

The free-standing trees – golden robinia and catalpa – were chosen especially for their moderate size and for their tolerance of town pollution. They will not grow too large for their allotted spaces. The flowering cherry, *Prunus subhirtella* 'Autumnalis', is another excellent small tree for restricted spaces, producing its dainty white

▼ **Children's playground** A secret hideaway is created in one corner by a dense screen of tough shrubs and perennials. They include New Zealand flax (*Phormium*), variegated dogwood (*Cornus alba* 'Elegantissima'), a slim juniper and bold *Euphorbia characias*. Honeysuckle covers the fence, and on the ground a layer of forest bark protects young knees from grazes.

or pink flowers during mild spells in late autumn and winter.

Along the fence are trained espalier and fan fruit trees and bushes, including apples, pears, peaches and the sour Morello cherry which grows well in a north-facing aspect. In limited spaces, it is advisable to plant self-fertile, or compatible, varieties in order to be sure of getting a good crop when the young trees start to bear fruit.

Blackberries, which prefer a slightly acid soil, are also trained against the fence and tied in to wires. They are the self-fertile thornless varieties and look attractive with their lush foliage hiding the wooden fence.

An ornamental grape vine, *Vitis vinifera* 'Brandt', growing against the house, adds brilliant pink, crimson and orange autumn leaf colour, although its sour, small red purple fruits don't appear regularly.

A fragrant rosemary hedge is planted in the low wall that surrounds the dining area. Evergreen and long-lived, rosemary tends to sprawl with age, but it responds well to pruning, in the early spring, as long as the old wood is not cut.

The raised bed could also be used to contain a miniature herb garden – lemon balm, thyme, basil, purple-leaved sage and

▲ **House climbers** Tucked into a corner against the house, two vigorous climbers enjoy each other's company. They take up little ground space, where the roots are in shade, but quickly cover the sunny upright support with leafy stems and purple clematis flowers and the long orange-red tubes of the Chilean glory flower (*Eccremocarpus scaber*). In mild winters, the latter is evergreen.

◄ **Centrepiece** Beneath the handsome canopy of an Indian bean tree (*Catalpa bignonioides*), a curved bench repeats the circular design of the garden. Creeping thyme grows among the cracks and lady's mantle (*Alchemilla mollis*) droops its green flowers over the edges. Set on well-weathered bricks, the view is towards the ornamental part of the garden.

marjoram. Rue and tansy have exceptionally strong scents, but are not to everyone's taste.

There is a roughly equal balance of evergreen and deciduous plants, so the garden has appeal even in winter. Ivy, escallonia, elaeagnus, evergreen climbing honeysuckle (*Lonicera japonica), Viburnum davidii*, silver privet, hebe and several dwarf junipers provide an all-year-round backdrop for various herbaceous perennials, deciduous shrubs and

climbers, and several fan-trained fruit trees.

Children in the garden
Planting has largely been confined to the boundary borders, leaving the centre open for play. The lawn is a hard-wear seed mixture that stands up to boisterous games; it will not be planted with naturalized bulbs for several years.

While children are still young, it is sensible to stick to tough

▲ **Family garden** Mature trees and evergreen foliage plants in this small urban garden create a sense of privacy as well as secret hiding places for young children.

plants and to avoid any with spiky or spiny leaves and stems. Several garden plants, including laburnum, lily-of-the-valley and yew berries, are poisonous and are better not introduced until the children are older.

CREATIVE PLANT DESIGNS

Imaginative use of foliage plants can transform the backyard of a terraced house into a miniature haven of tranquillity.

Planning and planting a very small town garden is often more difficult than creating a garden on a large plot. Its small size means that the whole can be taken in at a glance, which is quite a challenge at the planning stage.

Without a wide expanse of lawn, curving borders or a suggestion of secret areas, interest must be created by skilful use of plants and hard materials. Attention to detail is vital in the choice of plants and hard features, to give a series of miniature vignettes.

This tiny garden is an excellent example of small-scale planning. Level and almost square in shape, it is situated behind a brick-walled terrace town house which backs towards the south. Bounded by tall fences, the garden is too small for a lawn to make much sense. Instead, it is planned as an easily maintained paved garden with borders roomy enough for a good selection of plants.

The accent is on raised beds and a central platform, and on plants with strong shapes, textures and colours of foliage, though some also have attractive flowers.

Many of the shrubs are evergreen, and grey and silver foliage plays an important role. Several perennials keep their foliage all year so the garden has a well-furnished look in winter.

The flower colours are in soft, restful shades – bright colours could be overpowering in so small

---

▼ **Platform centrepiece** Raised borders and large gaps in the platform paving are filled with foliage plants and sprawling alpines. They enclose this small square town garden with walls of greenery and a floor of silvery-grey.

a space. And as the garden is a suntrap, cool shades rather than those from the warm part of the spectrum avoid too garish an effect.

York stone is used for the paving. As no two slabs are identical in size or tone, there is no hint of geometric monotony.

Boredom is also avoided by the inclusion of a raised, paved platform with gaps for plants. On one side of this is another bed, built on a slightly higher level.

The straight-edged boundary borders are also raised above the paving level. Because they occupy a small area it was easy to top up the impoverished soil with fresh, good quality topsoil.

The raised features give the impression that the paving is a sunken part of the garden – an excellent way of introducing variety to the basic small, square shape. Another benefit is that the raised plants – particularly smaller varieties – can be better appreciated.

Throughout, the choice of plants and their placing is managed so that the hard edges of the raised features are softened by plants billowing forward or down.

Foliage centrepiece

Plants grown in paving look extremely effective, but in a very small space greenery spilling everywhere may restrict movement. Here, on a raised platform, plants are displayed to advantage without getting in the way.

The varying shapes, textures and colours of plant foliage in the central bed provide interest during much of the year. Some of the plants have the additional advantage of seasonal flowers.

The dark green column of an Irish yew (*Taxus baccata* 'Fastigiata') placed near one corner makes a good vertical contrast to the low paving, and sets off the lighter shades of its platform associates. Its near neighbours are dwarf, yellow-flowered sisyrinchiums and the carpeting grey rosettes of *Antennaria parvifolia*.

Among the other plants – all with interesting foliage – in this raised paved area are the soft, grey-leaved semi-hardy trailer *Helichrysum petiolatum*, and the tender *Echeveria glauca* with blue-grey succulent rosettes. Other attractive foliage includes the blue-grey leaves of the sprawling *Euphorbia myrsinites*, and

A good view from the house – both from the ground floor and upper storeys – was an important planning consideration. Exotic, half-hardy plants thrive in the shelter of the house wall

Delicate forms and colours of flowers and foliage work well in small, sunny spaces with no grass-green colours to tone down bright shades. Pale and light colours give a feeling of open space

Plants in pots are moved from time to time, to display the flowers or give them extra light or shelter. This introduces flexibility to the design: even a slight change in arrangement can make a tiny garden look quite different

A sense of seclusion — essential in a town garden — is provided by climbers and shrubs at the boundaries. They are all of slender open habit, which avoids a jungle-like effect

N

The mellow paving is quiet in tone so as to emphasize the restful mood. The addition of the central platform and raised beds at the boundaries suggests a sunken surround

Changes of level add interest to the small, square shape of a town garden. Raised beds are ideal for bringing low-growing rock-garden plants closer to eye-level

the white-backed leaves of pink-flowered annual gazanias.

The central platform is raised to a higher level at one end, creating a bed for shrubs chosen for their foliage colours. The difference in levels adds welcome height and overcomes the problem of a flat-looking focal point. As the shrubs grow to maturity, they are pruned to shape or removed entirely to make room for different plants, thus giving scope for new foliage and colour combinations.

The sword-like leaves of a purple-leaved variety of New Zealand flax (*Phormium tenax*) make a strong vertical feature in this bed. A stronger purple comes from the leaves of a plum-coloured

▶ **Boundary cover** With its roots firmly anchored in shady soil, the vigorous clematis 'Comtesse de Bouchaud' clothes the trellis-topped fence with a mass of rose-pink, golden-eyed blooms through the summer, almost obscuring an everlasting pea.

◀ **Foliage contrast** A sunny house wall shelters the silver-grey filigree leaves of a semi-evergreen *Artemisia arborescens*. Unlikely to survive severe winters in the open, it has reached tree-like proportions here and contrasts dramatically with the imposing white and purple flower spikes of bear's breeches (*Acanthus mollis*).

smoke tree (*Cotinus coggygria* 'Royal Purple'), in strong contrast to the soft silver-grey of *Senecio* 'Sunshine' growing alongside.

More purple foliage, from *Berberis thunbergii* 'Atropurpurea Nana', is backed by the striped leaves of gardener's garters (*Phalaris arundinacea* 'Picta'). The colour scheme is repeated in the raised border with the orange-red flowers of *Lilium* 'Enchantment' and Peruvian lily (*Alstroemeria* 'Ligtu Hybrids').

Boundaries and borders
The boundaries of this secluded garden are thickly clothed with deciduous climbers and shrubs to mask the fence and to give agreeable views across the garden.

Climbers are strongly represented, including the large-flowered *Clematis* 'Comtesse de Bouchaud', whose shell-pink golden-centred blooms are charmingly associated with the white everlasting pea (*Lathyrus latifolius* 'White Pearl').

The large pure white flowers of *Clematis* 'Marie Boisselot' are particularly prominent at dusk. A large-leaved vine (*Vitis coignetiae*) covers a considerable space and contributes beautiful coloured autumn foliage.

Among border shrubs is the butterfly bush (*Buddleia davidii* 'Alba') whose long arching white plumes contrast with the rather flat pinkish lace-cap heads of a tall *Hydrangea sargentiana*. The glossy green, gold-variegated leaves of *Elaeagnus pungens* 'Maculata' and the white-splashed foliage of the dogwood *Cornus alba* 'Elegantissima' light up darker places.

In less sunny spots are peren-

▲ **Planting pockets** Gaps in the raised platform bed are planted with low-growing foliage plants. Purple-leaved bugle (*Ajuga reptans* 'Atropurpurea') creeps along the cracks, mingling with grey-leaved trailing *Helichrysum petiolatum* and silvery leaf rosettes of echeverias. An Irish yew stands like a green punctuation mark in one corner, coloured with pink gazanias and yellow evening primroses.

▲ **Sun revellers** The evergreen house-leek (*Sempervivum montanum*) creeps slowly along to form increasing low carpets of dark green leaf rosettes studded in summer with short stout stems of purple-pink flowers. It relishes full sun and any sharply-drained soil.

▼ **Leafy retreat** The mellow tones of paving and raised beds blend effectively with a wealth of foliage colours and textures. Subdued flower shades avoid any jarring note in the exuberance of leaf cover and come into their own when dusk falls.

▲ **Purple and silver** Strong leaf colours serve to highlight each other. The centrepiece in this dramatic association is an erect clump of purple-variegated *Phormium tenax* which rises above the near-circular leaves of *Cotinus coggygria* 'Royal Purple'. Fine contrast in texture, shape and colour comes from grey-green senecios and striped gardener's garters fronted by silvery-leaved *Convolvulus cneorum*.

nials which tolerate some shade. These include *Helleborus corsicus*, *Astrantia major*, hostas, including the variegated *Hosta undulata* 'Univittata' – all of which have attractive foliage – golden-flowered *Rudbeckia fulgida* and sweet-scented tobacco plants.

In more open, sunny situations are semi-shrubby *Euphorbia wulfenii*, woolly-leaved lamb's ear and silvery artemisias.

Another attractive feature of the garden is the careful placing of a few well-chosen pots. Their rounded outlines contrast with the straight lines of the paving, and the choice of plants complements the general scheme. Silvery grey artemisia foliage looks lovely against its terracotta container.

LOW-MAINTENANCE GARDENS

**Conifers and evergreen and deciduous shrubs
need little attention but furnish a garden with
colour and interest throughout the year.**

The garden described here has acquired a mature look in less than five years, mainly because a good selection of permanent planting in the form of trees and shrubs was made at the outset.

The small suburban garden, rectangular in shape and with acid soil, was planned for low maintenance and year-round interest. A surface of weathered bricks, laid in a herring-bone pattern, has replaced the traditional lawn area. A lawn would have worked just as well in this particular planting scheme, but it does require mowing and edging and, in a small garden, it usually needs nourishing at frequent intervals to compensate for hard and constant wear.

The simple paving scheme of light-coloured bricks for most of the plot creates an excellent plain setting for the plants. The intricate shapes and textures of the leaves can be appreciated against the uncluttered, flat surface. Low retaining walls are made of the same kind of bricks as those used for paving, so giving the garden coherence. The use of large quantities of brick in an intricate pattern can be costly and time-consuming to build, but a very similar effect can be achieved by using cheaper, more easily laid concrete paving slabs.

The curved shape of the paved area disguises the conventional, rectangular plot, giving it immediate interest. The addition of a circular island bed, set off-centre, helps to break up the basic shape even more and prevents the eye from taking in all the garden at once. It also does much to soften the effect of a large expanse of hard surface.

For a more mellow effect, small, prostrate, mound-forming plants can be squeezed into crevices between the bricks, or some bricks can be removed to make room for 'paving creepers' such as *Arabis*, saxifrages and thyme. Other paving plants with showy flowers, such as *Campanula, Dianthus* and *Raoulia*, would break up the rigid appearance of the rectangular brick paving even more.

▼ **Paved flooring** Brick paving forms a pleasing background for rich evergreen foliage. Prostrate shrubs, such as *Cedrus libani* 'Nana', creeping junipers, box and *Euonymus fortunei* 'Emerald 'n' Gold' keep weed growth to a minimum.

Designing with evergreens

In this garden, the planting relies heavily on conifers – mostly junipers and cypresses. They have been used with a definite style to provide a basic substance and form. Taller specimens have been planted around the edges which, besides creating privacy and shelter, also gives the boundary an interesting shape.

The two prominent Monterey cypresses (*Cupressus macrocarpa*) are fast-growing species that quickly form a good hedge or windbreak. Their bright yellow foliage and strong upright shape are offset by a columnar *Thuja orientalis* which tends to assume a more rounded outline with age.

To add to the variety of shapes and different tones of green, there is a Lawson's cypress (*Chamaecyparis lawsoniana*) near the house. Its drooping sprays of rich green, aromatic foliage take on a beautiful reddish glow in spring from a profusion of crimson catkins.

Completing the picture, the rear boundary is marked by the conical outline of a group of junipers. They are dark green and have small, dark berry-like cones.

Coniferous trees come into their own in winter. Their great advantage is that, unlike deciduous trees, they retain their leaves throughout the coldest months, always look good and can be appreciated all year round.

When coniferous trees are planted in groups, as they are here, their great diversity of texture, form, shape and colour shows to best effect. The 'strength' of conifer planting is particularly noticeable when they are associated with deciduous trees and shrubs, either intermixed or used as a dominant background.

The nature and characteristics of the two groups of trees – coniferous and deciduous – complement each other and have been used to good effect. At the rear of the garden, a mature whitebeam (*Sorbus aria*) effectively screens off the neighbouring garden. Few trees can surpass the beauty of whitebeam in autumn when its leaves turn russet and gold and its huge clusters of berries deepen to crimson.

Half-way along the western boundary, a purple-leaved cherry plum (*Prunus cerasifera* 'Pissardii') gives similar privacy, and continuous pleasure from early

▲ **Green boundaries** The design of this small, easily managed garden is deliberately architectural, with form and outline of primary importance. Curving beds and borders obscure the actual shape, and changes in surface levels and plant heights give an illusion of space and depth.

◄ **Carefree shrubs** A curved bed close to the patio is planted with evergreen shrubs that largely look after themselves. Azaleas maintain their glossy foliage the year round and burst into vivid bloom in late spring. Creeping junipers and trailing ivy eliminate the need for serious weeding, and honeysuckle covers the boundary fence.

124

spring when it is covered in a mass of pink-budded white flowers and the young dark red leaves mature to deep purple.

Dwarf and slow-growing conifers have been used in conjunction with the tree and shrub elements of the planting. They are an asset for their shape and texture alone. For example, *Thuja occidentalis* 'Rheingold', a slow-growing specimen that will eventually reach a height of only 3m (10ft), has a broadly conical outline with amber-gold foliage that is especially distinctive in winter. It contrasts boldly with the rich green conifers and other plants such as the hebes and junipers behind it.

Some of the trees, particularly the willow (*Salix*) in the island bed and the box (*Buxus sempervirens* 'Aurea') have been heavily clipped

into rounded topiary shapes in order to give the garden a formal feel.

Ground cover
Plenty of prostrate, mat-forming species of conifers, such as *Juniperus horizontalis*, *Cedrus libani* 'Nana' and the deciduous, red-berried *Cotoneaster horizontalis* have been used to cover the soil and create a thick, lush effect at ground level. They are spaced out around the borders, near the house and in the farthest corners of the garden so that it never looks bare, not even in the depths of the winter.

The shrub border
Shrubs, above all, are practical plants. Once settled, they look after themselves, needing only a minimum of training and pruning

to keep them shapely, healthy and within bounds. Yet when choosing border shrubs you are always faced with the problem of time – shrub gardening is future gardening. A period of at least five years is required before the infant, individual shrubs crowd together to make a fully-grown garden. In the meantime, short-lived perennials or annuals and bedding plants can be used to fill the gaps.

However, there are certain 'instant' shrubs that grow to almost full size in a mere two or three years and some of these, such as rock roses, buddleia and ceanothus, have been used here to give the appearance of maturity. Vigorous shrubs such as these usually bear a profusion of flowers and have a ready willingness to root from cuttings. Flowering currants, mock oranges and almost all willows come into the same useful category of quick-growing shrubs.

Seasonal value
One of the most reliable and important contributions that shrubs make to a garden is their combination of flowers, leaves and highly coloured fruit which are displayed at different times of the year. Shrubs in this garden have been carefully chosen to provide a year-round display of one form or another. It is in a continuous state of development, one shrub coming into bloom as another one fades.

The flowering season starts in mid spring when the gracefully arching stems of the evergreen *Berberis darwinii* flare into a vivid orange flower display, and the azaleas come into bloom. They have been deliberately planted near the house where they can be best appreciated.

Farther back, towards the rear of the garden, small white pitcher-shaped flowers are carried in drooping clusters on the glossy-leaved *Pieris japonica*. The deep green background of conifers makes its flowers seem like sparkling jewels. The shapely *Genista lydia* forms a hummock of piercing

◀ **Ground-cover plants** The vigorous *Hypericum calycinum* grows quickly to form a solid carpet that glows with golden-yellow flowers over many months. Flowering dead-nettle spreads equally quickly and its variegated leaves contrast pleasingly with prostrate juniper and small-leaved ivy.

treated as equal partners in a scene where all plant types shelter and complement each other.

Interspersed among the shrubs are the long, sword-like leaves of irises, and, in the island bed, the slender forms of lilies and ornamental grasses complement the bushy habits of evergreen shrubs. Bulbs are at home under low ground cover and in spring, snowdrops, winter aconites and daffodils look spectacular bursting through the mats of ivy.

Small clumps of annuals and bedding plants – mainly pinks, tobacco plants and geraniums – add colour and texture to the variety of evergreens in the borders. Hanging baskets near the house and strategically placed pots give seasonal colour.

◄ **Foliage colours** A small rock garden displays a range of evergreen leaf colours. The pale leaves of yellow-flowered creeping Jenny (*Lysimachia nummularia*) blend with the variegated foliage of *Euonymus fortunei* and the reddish *Epimedium × rubrum*.

yellow in spring. Other early flowering shrubs that would create a similar effect at this time of year are the flowering quinces, flowering currants, mahonias and daphnes.

The structurally handsome *Cornus controversa* flowers in late spring and early summer, and goes on to produce interesting blue-black berries in the autumn at the same time as the foliage turns purple-red before falling. The hebes reach the peak of their long flowering season in late summer, as do the fuchsias and the buddleias.

The evergreen *Elaeagnus pungens* 'Maculata' is a large, robust shrub that assumes importance during the winter months. Its large, dark green, silver-backed leaves are distinctively marked with a bold golden splash and it bears silvery flowers in late autumn.

Besides being used as a backdrop, the shrubs have been integrated with other plants. Herbaceous perennials, bulbs and annuals have been planted between the main masses and

► **Island bed** A grafted pussy willow (*Salix caprea* 'Kilmarnock') is the focal point in this bed. In late winter, it looks stunning with its drooping silvery and gold catkins.

N

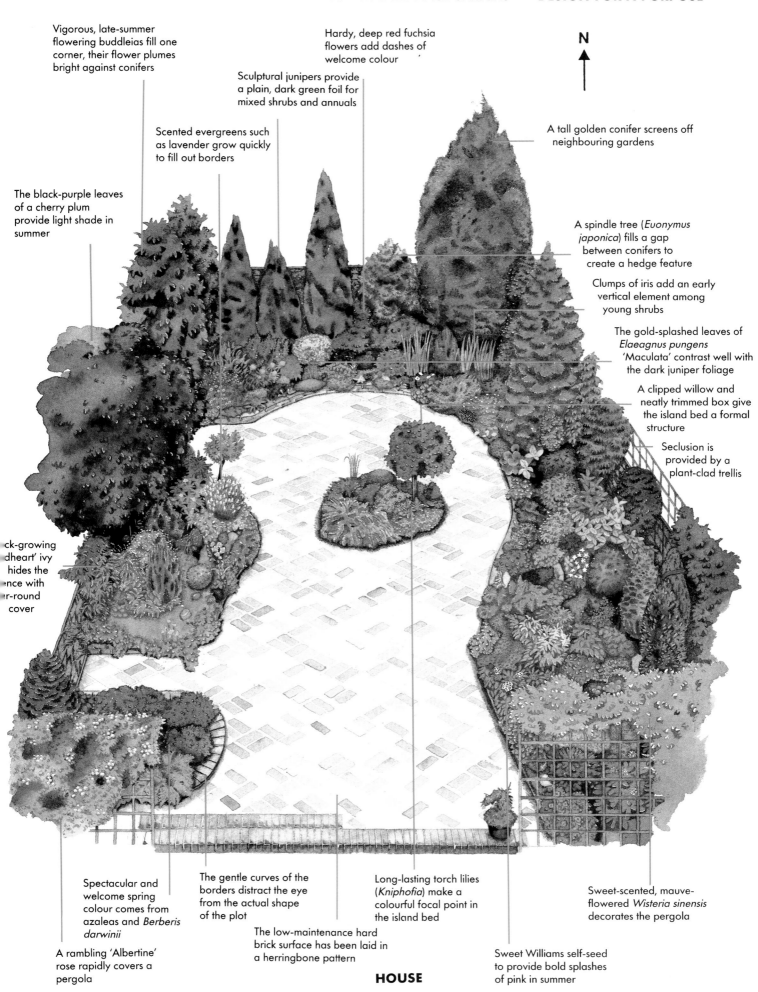

Vigorous, late-summer flowering buddleias fill one corner, their flower plumes bright against conifers

Hardy, deep red fuchsia flowers add dashes of welcome colour

Sculptural junipers provide a plain, dark green foil for mixed shrubs and annuals

Scented evergreens such as lavender grow quickly to fill out borders

A tall golden conifer screens off neighbouring gardens

The black-purple leaves of a cherry plum provide light shade in summer

A spindle tree (*Euonymus japonica*) fills a gap between conifers to create a hedge feature

Clumps of iris add an early vertical element among young shrubs

The gold-splashed leaves of *Elaeagnus pungens* 'Maculata' contrast well with the dark juniper foliage

A clipped willow and neatly trimmed box give the island bed a formal structure

Seclusion is provided by a plant-clad trellis

ck-growing dheart' ivy hides the nce with r-round cover

Spectacular and welcome spring colour comes from azaleas and *Berberis darwinii*

The gentle curves of the borders distract the eye from the actual shape of the plot

Long-lasting torch lilies (*Kniphofia*) make a colourful focal point in the island bed

Sweet-scented, mauve-flowered *Wisteria sinensis* decorates the pergola

A rambling 'Albertine' rose rapidly covers a pergola

The low-maintenance hard brick surface has been laid in a herringbone pattern

Sweet Williams self-seed to provide bold splashes of pink in summer

HOUSE

▲ **Scented canopy** A wooden pergola extending across the sunken patio will in time be completely covered by wisteria on one side and the rambling 'Albertine' rose on the other. Meanwhile, hanging baskets of bedding plants provide seasonal colour.

From the patio the neighbouring gardens are screened out by dense boundary planting, and the curving lines of the design invite closer inspection of specimens in the far corners.

▶ **Space fillers** A young, pale-leaved mock orange (*Philadelphus coronarius* 'Aureus') in the foreground is nursed along in a gap in the mixed border, sheltered by the leaves of a hydrangea. When it has put on more growth, it will be moved to a permanent site where it can reach its ultimate size of 2.4m (8ft) and display its fragrant creamy-white flowers.

TROMPE L'OEIL

A number of deceits that realistically create illusions of space or hidden secrets can be used successfully in the smallest of gardens.

Trompe l'oeil is French for 'deceives the eye'. In gardening, it refers to the creation of illusions that make a garden seem larger or more interesting than it is, to produce an example of beauty, or just to play a light-hearted joke.

The size of a garden largely determines the nature of the deceits. On huge English country estates, for example, the house and main gardens are often separated from grazing land by means of a steep-sided, large sunken ditch, or 'ha-ha' – so called after the sound of surprise made on discovering the 'invisible' boundary. A ha-ha allows the landscape to flow seemingly unbroken before the eye, while preventing cattle, sheep or deer from ruining lawns and flower beds.

Follies are another visual trick of grand estates – purpose-built 'ruined' castles and classical temples scaled down to create a false perspective and an increased sense of distance, as well as to inspire dreamy or romantic feelings.

A carriage drive leading from the gate to the main entrance of a large country house often took roundabout routes, to give arriving guests the impression they were visiting a much larger estate than actually existed. 'Dummy' bridges were sometimes built on dry land adjacent to ornamental lakes to give the impression that the water extended farther than it did.

In most ordinary gardens, neither space nor finance allows for such sweeping gestures, but small-scale *trompe l'oeil* can be as effective and amusing, in its own way, as the extravagant tricks played on large landscapes.

Layout deceits

Concealing the boundaries of a small garden makes it seem bigger: dense shrubbery round the perimeter is the most effective solution. Breaking up the space, however small, is another visual deceit. Trellises, hedges, narrow beds or broad shrubberies that extend into the central area of a garden, for example, encourage the eye to imagine that the space beyond extends farther and wider than in reality.

Altering the symmetry of a garden can enhance the feeling of spaciousness – for example, a path curving gently rather than proceeding in a straight line; or one running along one side of the garden, rather than straight down the middle of the lawn.

Mirrors

More than any other object, mirrors create an illusion of space in a confined area, doubling whatever image they reflect. The corner of a garden, especially where the two 'legs' of an L-shaped garden meet, is suitable for such a trick – site the mirror so that the junction appears to offer a choice

◄ **Wall mural** Summer appears to linger in this elaborate *trompe l'oeil*. A false arch depicts a lush garden forever green, in contrast to the real garden in late-autumn mood.

of paths, one the real leg, the other its reflection. A blank wall is another possible location, or immediately behind a feature, such as a statue or pool.

Setting a mirror at an angle to the viewer is usually more effective than setting it straight on, because as soon as you can see your own reflection approaching, the illusion of additional space is destroyed.

As well as being angled to reflect another part of the garden, periscope style, a mirror should ideally reflect a light, bright, image, rather than a dark one: a bit of sky, for example, or a sun-filled border.

A broad, unbroken expanse of mirror is less convincing than one which is slightly obscured. A flat trellis backed by a mirror is a very good combination, especially if climbers are encouraged to grow around it. Placing a mirror immediately behind a palisade gate, door- or window-shaped frame also helps the eye accept the trick, giving the illusion of space beyond. Even more effective is a mirror behind a three-dimensional trellis or ironwork arch, creating an enticing tunnel which the eye, if not the body, is invited to explore.

With semi-circular pools or raised brick seating areas backing on to a wall, a carefully placed, wall-hung mirror can complete the circle, doubling the size visually. Alternatively you could place a mirror a little below ground level, mask it slightly with foliage, and by reflecting the sky above create the illusion of a sunken pool.

Be wary of using too many mirrors. The infinitely receding tunnel of images created by reflecting one mirror within another quickly loses its amusement value. Indeed, multiple mirrors reproduce reflections so many times that they tend to give a garden a peculiarly crowded feel rather than a sense of increased space.

Outdoor mirrors, even more than those in bathrooms, are vulnerable to changes in temperature and humidity. Tell your supplier that the mirror is to be used ex-

▲ **Water sport** A roof garden, turned into a secluded, leafy pool, seems to have attracted a passing swan. A fountain sprays water at the sculpture's feet, realistically simulating the moment of impact, while hiding its mounting.

▲ ▶ **False perspective** Specially constructed trelliswork gives the impression of a pergola. Twining sprays of foliage and pots of flowering plants, arranged at the base of the trellis, add credibility to the deceit.

▶ **Conjuring trick** Topsy-turvy planting, painting and trelliswork all help to confuse the eye. A real trellis, erected in front of a wall, supports plants at right angles while others hang in front of a *trompe l'oeil* trellis complete with small statue.

ternally; it must be heavy duty, at least 6mm (¼in) thick, and lead backed to protect against corrosion. A mirror that is sheltered from drips by overhanging roof eaves, wall coping or trellis is likely to last longer than one completely exposed to the elements. Lastly, a mirror makes a positive contribution only when clean, so allow reasonable access to it.

Murals

Paintings of leafy scenes, landscapes or lofty architecture to create a feeling of airy perspective in a confined space is a form of *trompe l'oeil* that goes back at least as far as the Romans. As a refuge from the intense heat of the Mediterranean summer, Livia,

the wife of Augustus Caesar, had a very cool, underground, barrel-vaulted room built. The inside was painted to look like a beautiful, balustraded garden, complete with ornamental trees, shrubs, flowers and even birds. In Roman town houses, courtyards had frescoes depicting trees and flowers to give an increased sense of space.

In today's urban and suburban gardens, the white-painted walls of basement areas or over-shadowed urban gardens can be decorated with realistic or imaginative landscapes or plants as sparsely or densely as taste, time and budget allow.

Decide at the outset whether the mural should be flat and simplified, in the manner of a stencil, or

▲ **Tricks of the trade** Huge urns vanish into a stylized background. Although the painting makes no attempt to trick the eye, real urns in front of it reinforce the three-dimensional impression of movement out of the picture and towards the spectator.

▶ **Mirror images** A tiny basement garden appears twice the size after a huge mirror has been attached to a white-painted wall. Trellis and climbing clematis help the illusion. Mirrors work best when they are hung to reflect still life — movement tends to shatter any reflection from the glass.

three-dimensional, which involves perspective, a vanishing point and shadows. Flat images can be decorative, but are less effective as visual deceits. Three-dimensional images, such as buildings, an avenue of trees or balustrades receding into the distance, are more difficult to do well, but potentially more effective at creating a feeling of depth and spaciousness. Consider hiring a professional artist, since a poorly executed scheme is far worse than a straightforward, white-painted wall.

As with mirrors, murals are especially effective on end walls, which otherwise define the limits of a garden. Blank walls opposite windows or French doors overlooking the garden are also suitable and can be enjoyed indoors as well as out. You needn't paint the entire wall: a small *trompe l'oeil* 'window' in a wall, giving a painted view of a pool with sprinkling fountain or of rolling countryside with tree-lined avenues 'beyond', would be delightful.

Consult a professional artist about the type of paint suitable for

▶ **Illusions of space** A mirrored archway creates an impression of an inviting garden beyond the conifer screen. Made from a single sheet of tough glass, the mirror needs frequent cleaning to maintain the illusion.

external murals; priming, water-proofing and even re-rendering of the wall may be necessary before-hand.

Trellis, hedges and fences

Arched, wooden wall-trellises are available with built-in false per-spectives – a central, eye-level vanishing point towards which the upper battens radiate. Such trellises are more effective hung against a plain or rendered wall than a brick one, whose own paral-lel and right-angled lines are counterproductive. And though some softening effect from foliage and flowers is desirable, heavy, lush growth tends to obscure the deceit of the trellis.

Another trick is to have hedges clipped and fences built to become lower the farther from the house they go, but this is effective only when done gradually, and on a scale larger than the ordinary gar-den. If done over a short distance, the angle has to be sharp to be effective, and the eye would com-pare it with other, naturally re-ceding lines, such as those of nearby hedges, walls or roofs. The contradiction would be bizarre.

Sculpture

There are several ways of using sculpture as *trompe l'oeil*; all re-quire firm foundations and fixings, so that the statues remain perfectly upright and secure. Most also re-quire a large amount of time and money, since *trompe l'oeil* statuary is not mass produced.

Before embarking on such a pro-ject, remember that a witty sculp-ture could lose its charm if you are endlessly exposed to it. Ideally, you need to store the sculptures and take a break from the joke from time to time.

You can treat the garden like a front-facing stage and build 'flats' – wood, marine-grade plywood or chipboard cut-outs painted to look three-dimensional, and supported from behind with wooden struts, as on film sets. Suitable subjects might be classical stone statues or columns, ruins and, if patience allows, animals such as a grazing horse or even a flock of geese.

The drawback is fairly obvious: like a front-facing stage, the trick only works when seen straight on; a sideways view exposes the object as a cut-out fake. It is best to site flats at the very end of a garden and to back the 'statue' with shrubs or other plants to help con-ceal the supporting framework.

Three-dimensional statues that pretend to look real – life-sized and realistically painted moulded sheep for example – take the *trompe l'oeil* one stage further. On a smaller scale a grey stone cat could forever perch in a tree or on a roof; or a bronze water bird could be always landing on the surface of a pool, with perhaps a small fountain spray of water to simu-late the moment of landing.

Colour

Painting a wall in pale colours or white gives the impression that the wall is closer than it is. Paint-ing the same wall with dark colours makes it seem farther away. You can use white, black and any colour to change the visual impression of an area. In a long, narrow garden, for example, planting a white border at the far end will make it seem closer to the eye; in a short, wide garden, plant-ing the end bed with dark-coloured flowers has the opposite effect, pushing it visually back-wards. Again, as with the parallel lines of a hedge or fence, the larger the space the more effective it is.

A post or trellis on a wall – even a change in the material the wall is made of – will interrupt the eye, giving the impression of a smaller plane. By painting everything in one single colour – including the interruptions – it's possible to 'stretch' the surface.

◄ **Trick upon trick** A symmetrical trellis on a plain wall draws the eye inwards to its vanishing point – a mirror reflection of another trellis opposite. The illusion is completed with trick planting – plastic holly adorns the arches in the trellis.

Theme gardens

Certain situations call for particular designs. Garden size, surrounding landscape, soil type, time and many other factors place constraints on a design, but these need not be unnecessarily constricting. Roof gardens, for example, are unalterable in size, demand shelter from the sun and wind-resistant plants. But within these limitations and those posed by the load-bearing capacity of the roof itself, there are numerous options for creating miniature landscapes among the clouds.

In an open and sunny situation, design flair may envisage a formal garden surrounded by red-tiled walls and filled with earthy colours reminiscent of the Mediterranean regions of southern Europe. Shade, on the other hand, need not be a barrier to good garden design. Shady sites suit many layouts, from classical knots and parterres, to water gardens of oriental splendour and formal designs which include topiary, clipped hedges and geometric stone features.

An alpine landscape can be created on a rocky site, with the help of exquisite dwarf conifers, and some of our most brightly coloured flowers, while from the other side of the world, traditional Japanese gardens capture the essence of nature herself. Rocks and water are their inspiration, with trees and shrubs chosen for their form and colour to add depth and perspective to small spaces.

On top of the world Wind-resistant shrubs and climbers transform a rooftop garden into a sheltered oasis.

ROOF GARDENS

**High-level gardens make ideal outdoor
rooms for relaxation and entertaining, furnished
with tough, wind-resistant plants.**

Roof gardening is far from easy and takes a lot of careful planning. However, the end result is usually well worth the effort – a compact and charming garden among gable-ends and chimney pots and the possibility of growing a wide range of plants in troughs and containers.

Gardening among the clouds presents different problems from those encountered at ground level. It is essential that the roof structure is solid enough to take the combined weight of soil, containers and plants, and provision must be made for proper drainage – plants grown in confined spaces and exposed to the full force of sun and wind dry out quickly.

The garden described here is a real aerial backyard, perched half way up a block of flats with breathtaking views over the city. It works as a genuine 'outdoor room'.

The structure

The roof area measures approximately 3.5 × 5m (12 × 16ft) – the size of an average room inside the house. The starting point for the design is a crisp no-nonsense floor of lightweight tiles which, besides providing unobtrusive flooring and background, also allows water to drain away quickly to gutters behind the surrounding parapet walls.

A contrasting material of thin natural stone slabs has been used in one corner, adjoining the flat – this change in texture raises the floor level slightly and defines an area for a small group of pots.

The parapet walls to either side have been topped with a simple but practical frosted glass screen. This provides shelter from the wind – important in a roof garden – and also privacy from the garden next door.

The screen consists of squared timber to support panes of ample

▶ **High-rise gardening** Open to sky, sun and wind, this rooftop garden is an oasis of green foliage and colourful summer bedding, with views over the city landscape.

size; they echo the style of the adjoining window, reinforcing the link between inside and out. Frosted glass has proved a good choice, because it creates soft reflections that enhance the planting in the border below.

The parapet wall is wide enough to accommodate planting troughs specially constructed to fit neatly between the uprights of the screen. The troughs are deep enough for ample planting, giving extra privacy at a slightly higher level than might otherwise have been possible.

The centre of the garden has been left almost completely clear – happily, it faces almost due south. A few containers have been placed on the wall in order to break up the long horizontal line. This, however, is a real hazard and best avoided – gusts of wind can easily

◄ **Container planting** Backed by tough glass windscreens, bedding plants spill over the edges of troughs and boxes. Silvery helichrysum and blue lobelias tumble beneath white marguerites and red fuchsia bells.

▼ **Spring colour** Evergreen foliage shrubs shelter a mass of spring bulbs — hyacinths, daffodils, narcissi and tulips, and the exotic china-pink blooms of camellias.

The roof garden is enclosed by waist-high parapet walls for safety and in order to create the feel of an outdoor room. Made from timber supports and frosted glass panes, they provide privacy and shelter from the wind, with only a slight loss of light

All planting is done in pots and containers filled with pre-packaged lightweight compost. At this altitude, sun and wind have a particularly drying effect, and watering may be necessary several times a day during summer

N

Planting at the outer parapet wall is kept deliberately low and compact, to give uninterrupted views out over the city. Evergreens ensure that the view, even in winter, is framed in colour

Lightweight floor tiles, close butted and waterproofed, provide a neutral background for the planting. Laid to slope slightly, surface water drains off the floor to gutters behind the parapet walls

knock over the pots and send them over the edge to crash on to the ground below.

Container planting

All planting has been done in containers – wooden troughs, fibreglass bowls, terracotta and plastic pots and boxes. Heavy containers should be avoided, for weight reasons. At the same time there is a danger of small light pots being knocked over by the wind; they also inhibit growth and dry out quickly.

The prime task of any planting scheme is to provide colour and interest throughout the year. This garden is wrapped round with a backdrop of permanent shrub planting, combining evergreen and deciduous species.

A stag's-horn sumach (*Rhus typhina*) is by far the largest of the

▶ **Tropical touches** Pots of cabbage palm (*Cordyline australis*) make strong accent points among spring-flowering bulbs. Slow-growing, these striking evergreen shrubs rarely exceed 90cm (3ft) in height.

▼ **Background greenery** Canary Island ivy and ornamental vines clothe the house walls. Honeysuckle and summer jasmine fill the air with their sweet scent. A Chusan palm displays its leaf fans in their shade.

▲ **Specimen shrubs** Stag's horn sumach makes an arresting focal point. Huge, pale red flower clusters in summer turn to russet seed heads by autumn and persist long after the orange-red leaves have fallen.

◄ **Conifer columns** Close to the house wall, a Chinese juniper forms a conical shape of dense grey-green foliage, soothing against the brightness of summer annuals.

deciduous shrubs and makes a splendid specimen with its architectural shape and foliage. In many ways this is an ideal tub plant as it has the annoying tendancy to throw out suckers when planted in the open garden.

Evergreens are well represented. Two varieties of palm are on display – the fan-shaped leaves of the Chusan or Chinese windmill palm (*Trachycarpus fortunei*) being particularly effective.

The cabbage palm (*Cordyline australis*) also makes a strong impact. It is an ideal pot plant, being slow-growing and tolerant of wind exposure. Generally hardy, it may need to be moved indoors during severe winter weather. Yuccas are equally tough and do well on sunny roof gardens.

Camellias, too, are superb container plants and their glossy evergreen leaves are a welcome sight, especially in winter. They do best in light shade; avoid siting the containers in east-facing positions where the early-spring flowers are easily spoiled by morning sun after night frost.

Conifers provide additional evergreen interest; dwarf and miniature junipers and false cypresses are ideal for container-growing. Winter-flowering heathers are especially welcome during the dullest months.

The Mexican orange blossom (*Choisya ternata*) is a useful evergreen with pretty, white scented flowers appearing in late spring and early summer. Honeysuckle and jasmine scramble their way up the brickwork, softening the building's flat lines. Many honeysuckles are semi-evergreen, particularly on a warm roof, which makes them a sensible choice. An attractive fruiting vine (*Vitis vinifera*) also grows up the house.

Bulbs, including crocuses, narcissi and hyacinths, are the first to flower, followed later by pots of regal lilies and summer bedding – a vibrant display of pelargoniums, busy Lizzies (*Impatiens*), trailing lobelia, marigolds and fresh white Marguerite daisies. Annuals are used extensively to provide instant colour from spring through to autumn.

Many of the shrubs are Mediterranean in origin – grey-leaved types such as senecio, phlomis and helichrysum. Sun lovers, such as potentillas, cistus, hebe and hibiscus revel here, and many herbs will enjoy the same aspect and thrive in dry soil. In shade, ivies and the tough evergreen elaeagnus are unrivalled.

PLANNING ROOF GARDENS

The first thing to consider when planning a roof garden is the safety and suitability of the roof in question. Weight will be a major consideration – anyone contemplating a roof garden should be aware that pots, containers, plants and soil (even lightweight soil) will place severe pressure on the structure below.

Always consult a surveyor, for while many newer buildings may be quite suitable, old timber roofs can present all kinds of problems. You will probably have to obtain planning permission from the Local Authority.

Adequate shelter is also very important – what may be a gentle breeze at street level could become a strong wind several floors up. In towns, the alignment of roofs and buildings may even give rise to unexpected draughts and eddies, which can make life unpleasant for plants and people alike. In any case, careful planning and the provision of shelter are absolutely vital if young plants are not to be scorched by sun and wind.

Shade is especially important if you want to sit outside for any length of time and it could well be worthwhile to construct overhead beams to form an open-framed roof. These will be ideal for fragrant climbing plants and can have the added bonus of screening the garden below from neighbours' windows. They will also be the perfect support for hanging baskets, provided there is adequate shelter.

In strong sunlight, timber will quickly dry out and preservative will have to be applied more often than usual. Roof gardens usually have little storage space and furniture will in all probability have to stand out throughout the year. It is best to keep this in mind when buying furniture sturdy enough for a roof garden.

Avoid using white paint, which can dazzle. Cream is ideal. Remember that the darker the colour, the more heat it will retain. This is rarely comfortable for an area that is in sun for much of the day.

▶ **Outdoor rooms** Shelter is all important for roof gardens – as protection from wind, sun and curious neighbours. Camouflaged by climbing plants, these walls are also attractive in their own right.

Lawn substitutes

Artificial grass can be laid like carpet over any flat surface and cut to a free-flowing pattern that provides a real feeling of space and movement. It genuinely looks like grass, but needs little attention and brings an undeniable softness to an urban situation where real grass is impractical.

Provided the roof is secure, with high enough walls or fences, artificial grass is also ideal for children to play on.

Optional extras

You may wish to incorporate built-in seating, raised beds or a small sunken pool. None of these is out of the question, as long as the surveyor gives the go-ahead on load-bearing capacity.

Water can be a particularly effective use of space, but it is nearly as heavy as soil and a conventional pool would have to be quite small. A glassfibre 'millstone' arrangement, fitted above a small tank, with water circulated by a submersible pump, to bubble over the 'stone' and back into the tank might be more effective and could provide an excellent focal point.

Water from a tap is in any event essential as regular irrigation and overhead spraying may both be needed morning and evening in hot, dry spells.

Exterior lighting is extremely useful, to extend the time you can use the garden. It is best to keep it simple: a few well positioned, unobtrusive fittings will look far more effective than imitation coachlamps or the holographic displays sold in some garden centres.

A roof garden may be an addition to a conventional ground-level plot or, in the case of flat-dwellers, the only available space. Although creating a roof garden may involve hard work initially, you will ultimately be able to enjoy a private green oasis in what was previously a barren space.

KNOT GARDENS

**Knot gardens have classical origins and a
noble history. Their geometric designs and topiary shapes
suit formal gardens, whatever their size.**

Enormous knot gardens in public parks and palaces can be impressive, but they may seem somewhat irrelevant to the everyday garden planning of an average, modest-sized plot.

In fact, knot gardens – clipped edging plants arranged in formal, geometric patterns – can fit readily into ordinary gardens. They may be the dominant feature, as with this delightful knot garden, or form one focal point of a larger, varied layout.

Knot gardens are especially suitable for small urban gardens, such as this one, which have flat, featureless plots and right-angled boundaries. Instead of concealing or camouflaging such restrictions, knot gardens take advantage of them, emphasizing the level surface and embellishing the formal geometry.

Most urban houses have at least two storeys, and knot gardens – designed initially as plans – are at their best looked down on from above: the higher, the better.

Site and layout

This long, thin garden backs on to an urban terrace house and is bounded on three sides by walls. Immediately outside the house is a paved sitting area, with garden furniture and potted plants.

A lozenge-shaped knot garden, laid out on a central axis and divided crossways in half, extends over most of the remaining area. The two halves form a mirror image, and are in themselves symmetrical. A classical stone urn on a plinth marks the centre of the knot garden.

Within the simple outlines are elegant curves, arabesques and cruciforms of box, tightly grouped to form larger ornamental patterns. Bare earth in the remaining space emphasizes the sculptural

▶ **Small-scale knot garden**
Immaculately clipped box in a geometric design gives unique character to a narrow town garden. An overhead tunnel of laburnum lifts the view up and above the flat plan.

quality of the box, and allows the geometry to be seen clearly and without interruption.

Narrow brick paths edge both long sides of the knot garden and separate it from narrow borders along the boundary walls. The long beds contain informal mixed shrub and ground-cover planting, while retaining the garden's formal, architectural overtones.

Beyond the knot garden is an island bed set in an area of gravel; like the long borders, it is informally planted.

Borrowed landscape consists of overhanging laburnums from adjacent gardens. Together, the trees create a small-scale imitation of the ornamental tree tunnels which were popular at the time of the first knot gardens.

The formality of a knot garden demands rigorous upkeep. One of the most important tasks is pruning the box edging, which has to be cut back fairly hard each year in early spring.

Weeding is also important, to maintain the flat plane of bare soil within the knot design – an invasion of weeds would spoil the clarity of line. Chemical weedkilling in spring is combined with hand weeding of persistent offenders to keep the ground clear.

Hard landscaping

Path and paving details are simple and unobtrusive. The paving material consists of old-fashioned narrow paving bricks, laid tight-butted and close-jointed in a crossways stretcher bond. Laying the bricks crossways, like dividing the knot garden in half crossways, helps to counteract the restriction of a long, narrow space. The paths merge into gravel at the far end.

The central stone urn is also surrounded by gravel, its pale colour contrasting with the green of the box.

Box edging

The dwarf box (*Buxus sempervirens* 'Suffruticosa') is the traditional choice for knot gar-

◄ **Summer highlights** The intricate scrolls and flowing arabesques of a knot garden are fully appreciated when viewed from above, each line and curve picked out in bright green. Scale can be adapted to suit gardens of all sizes, with a miniature version making a handsome centrepiece.

dens. A woody evergreen, it has a year-round presence which is especially valuable in winter.

Box is slow growing – so the task of clipping is more manageable – and responds well to pruning. It can be kept very short or left to reach its natural height of about 1.2m (4ft). Box is also long lived so will last for many years. It is equally happy in sun or shade, thrives in any kind of soil, and is relatively pest and disease free.

Though evergreen, box leaves display subtle seasonal changes. The young spring growth is a fresh pale green, in contrast to the dark green mature foliage, giving the plant a charming two-toned effect. And though not everyone enjoys the scent, box is aromatic.

General planting

In keeping with the formal theme, the knot garden is punctuated with four standard roses, planted symmetrically in the corners closest to the central urn. The urn is planted with small-leaved trailing ivies for winter interest, with flowering bulbs in spring and ivy-leaved pelargoniums to give colour for the rest of the year.

Informally planted ground-cover plants, including lamium, hosta, bergenia, ornamental grasses, irises and ferns fill the narrow borders by the boundaries, and the island bed. Modest ribbons of colour come from pink busy Lizzies edging the path.

Wisteria and clematis twine up the staircase and along the balcony, and climbing roses are trained along the boundary walls.

Features and focal points

The knot garden centres on a simple, classical stone urn. Immediately beyond the knot garden is another stone urn on a fluted column. At the other end, a large potted standard rose pleasantly reinforces the linear symmetry of the garden.

To add touches of colour and soften the formality a little, groups of terracotta flower pots hold seasonal bedding plants.

► **Winter spectacular** A knot garden in evergreen box is attractive throughout the year, but it looks truly magnificent with a dusting of frost or snow when the design reveals itself in simple formality. Box is fully hardy and responds well to regular clipping and topiary designs.

KNOT GARDEN DESIGNS

▲ ▼ **Square designs** Simple lines work well in knot-garden patterns. A square grid of plain green box, infilled with gravel, is punctuated with perfectly clipped spheres of golden box.

▼ **Diamond patterns** Ground cover plants – prostrate roses and nepetas – fill the spaces. Bedding plants such as busy Lizzies, wax begonias, ageratums and French marigolds could also be used.

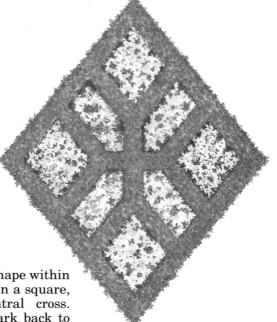

Getting started

A knot garden's pattern should be immediately obvious, or the overall effect will be lost. Experiment with graph paper, a pair of compasses and a set square.

Draw the area to scale, allowing 20cm (8in) for the width of box edging. For ornamental plant infill, leave more open space – say 45cm (1ft 6in) – than for bare earth or hard surfacing. It's easier to lay out and clip straight lines, circles or sections of circumference than arabesques.

Try one geometric shape within another: a circle within a square, perhaps with a central cross. Cross-shaped plans hark back to the two main allées of monastery gardens, and are as good a starting point as any. Try circles within circles or squares within squares. Diagonals can be used to create diamonds or triangles.

Simple designs are often the most effective, but if you feel ambitious consider a design that includes heraldic patterns or real or imaginary animals.

The first letter of your name could be worked into a geometric pattern; some letters, such as C, H, M, V, X, O, and Y, are symmetrical within themselves, and fit easily into a knot pattern.

When you are satisfied with the design, peg out the pattern on the soil. A peg with a piece of string attached can be used to give the circumference of a circle. For a small knot garden with gravel infill you could cover the area with perforated black plastic – which will help suppress weeds – then draw out the design and plant through the plastic before covering the surface with gravel.

Box should be spaced 23cm (9in) apart. Stocking up with plants from a garden centre is likely to be expensive, but you will have a garden feature of great character that could last for generations.

You can save on the initial cost by raising plants from box cuttings, obtained perhaps from a friend's or neighbour's prunings. Rooted in a cold frame in late summer, the cuttings should be grown on in a nursery bed for a couple of years before being planted out permanently.

You could also use lavender or santolina in a knot-garden design.

They are less formal in shape than box, but especially suitable for infills of herbs.

Knot-garden infill

In Tudor knot gardens, spaces between edging plants were filled with honesty, sweet William, pansy, narcissus, violet, rose, lily, marigold, columbine, primrose and cowslip. Sometimes they were planted with a mossy carpet of turf or low-growing herbs.

▶ **A knot of herbs** 'Hidcote' lavender is used to trace this Elizabethan design. Pots of sweet Cicely on a gravel base are grouped around a focal point of aromatic bay clipped to a pyramid shape.

Potager, the art of planting vegetables and herbs in decorative geometric patterns within low box hedges, was popular in the 16th century. Much later, the Victorians filled knot gardens with colourful summer annuals and tender bedding plants.

Infilling knot gardens with plants provides colour, fragrance

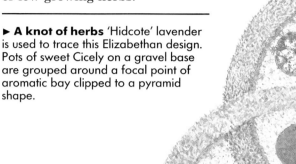

▼ **Circular theme** Triangular segments make up a traditional pattern. Centrepiece in the knot garden is a weeping standard rose, with the green and yellow theme repeated in infills of lady's mantle (*Alchemilla mollis*).

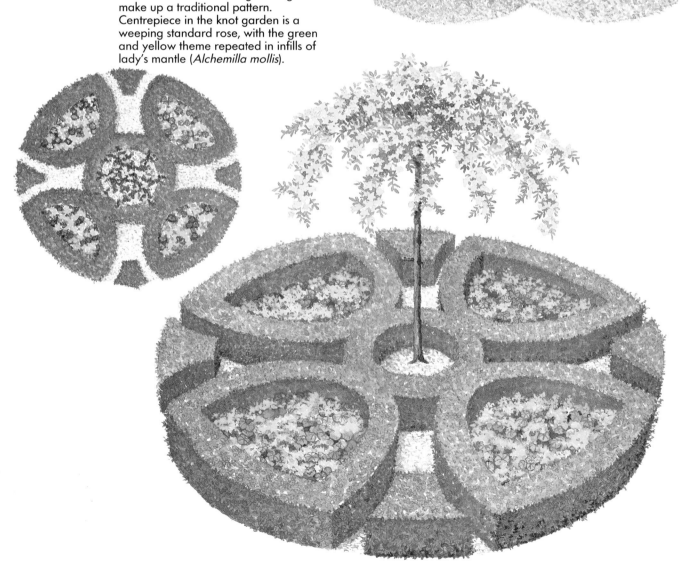

◄ **Centrepiece** The visual impact of a knot garden is heightened with a central vertical feature that rises above, yet unites the individual segments. The focal point can be a sundial, a clipped topiary specimen in box or yew, a piece of statuary or a tripod of roses.

Formal parterres in large country gardens often make a feature of intricate knot gardens arranged around a large water fountain – in the average garden, a bird bath would be in better keeping, or a simple urn filled with bright bedding plants.

Gravel is the traditional infill; it must be kept free of weeds so as not to obscure the outline of the design.

and seasonal interest, but the clarity of the design can be confused unless low-growing plants are used. Choose plants that can fend for themselves rather than those needing constant attention – working conditions are likely to be uncomfortably cramped.

Coloured sand, stones, earth, ashes, brick dust, tiles and chalk often replaced flowers in early knot gardens, to give flat, abstract patterns of colour. Purists even replaced the edging plants with wooden strips.

A modern version could be made, in a simple square or diamond pattern, using a selection of coloured concrete paving stones, gravel, interlocking concrete pavers or bricks.

Alternative edgings
Before box became popular, dwarf pungent herbs were used: lavender, thrift, rosemary, hyssop, mint, marjoram, santolina or thyme. Many were short lived and needed frequent clipping to remain compact – the clippings were often used for strewing on floors, to scent airless rooms.

If you don't mind the extra lift-ing, dividing, replanting and pruning involved, a herb-edged knot garden would be very pretty.

Introducing focal points
A vertical feature automatically enlivens a knot garden's low, flat plane of greenery. In a small knot garden, one central plant or ornament is enough; larger knot gardens can have several focal points, perhaps with slightly smaller features set in the corners.

Stone fountains are traditional, but sundials, birdbaths, statues, small stone seats, raised planters or urns all work well. Trellis (or 'carpenter's work' as it was called) was popular when knot gardens first became fashionable, and could make a pleasant feature.

Plants that are naturally columnar, or are trained or grafted into upright shapes, make good focal points: for example, junipers and Irish yews; standard bays, fuchsias and pelargoniums; and grafted standard roses and weeping cotoneasters.

Box and yew topiary make excellent focal points in a knot garden; as variations on the theme of formally clipped evergreen plants, they create a pleasantly unified, historical feel.

Historical footnote
Apart from the attraction of having a feature with such unique character in your garden, a knot garden gives a real sense of garden history. The earliest formal gardens of clipped plants were found in Roman times, and feature in many of the great and famous gardens of the world.

Medieval monastic herb gardens were subdivided into orderly rectangular beds, but more for practicality than beauty. The Renaissance, with its interest in classical culture, revived the art of clipped ornamental gardens.

From Italy, knot gardens spread to France, Holland and England. They remained popular until, in the 18th century, there was a return to a more natural style of garden – this was a reaction against the extreme examples of formal gardening, such as Versailles.

The Victorians loved knot gardening and many Victorian parks still have knot garden displays. Recently there has been a revival of interest in knot designs.

ORIENTAL WATER GARDENS

**Eastern garden designs contrast open spaces
with crowded areas, and stillness with movement in
order to create a mood of tranquillity.**

The finest gardens are more often than not a happy coincidence of a good site, a sympathetic eye and a genuine feel for plants. Just occasionally a designer sets out with a specific brief and achieves something quite special.

In this case an average suburban garden, neglected for a great many years, was transformed into a peaceful retreat with a definite Oriental feel. The design proves even a temperate climate garden can have a truly Eastern flavour.

Water is a special feature of the garden – as it nearly always is in the East. The centrepiece is a wedge-shaped pool that marvel-lously reflects the contrasting shapes of surrounding foliage. Timber decking, set at different levels and angles round the pool and sitting area, is reminiscent of the raised wooden houses of South-East Asia, while a movable collection of pot plants, subtle plant forms and delicate bamboo handrails augment the mood.

Materials used for the hard features have a natural, honest simplicity; they are handled with quiet confidence and precise attention to detail – stepping stones set in gravel, for instance, are sympathetic to the overall mood and thoroughly practical.

The brief

The initial task in garden design is a basic site appraisal. Here the plot is long and narrow – 25m (82ft) by 10m (33ft) – bounded by a road on one side and gardens on the other. Outbuildings stand at the bottom of the plot while the rear of the house faces north, casting shadow over the area nearest the house wall. The site is essentially flat, the boundaries rectangular.

▼ **Eastern atmosphere** A small suburban garden, enclosed by rush-covered screens, captures the essence of Oriental philosophy, with water, wood and plant form at its centre.

The brief was for a low maintenance garden that provided colour and interest throughout the year. The garden was to be given an essentially Oriental feel with a strong emphasis on water.

Ample room for sitting, dining and entertaining was a basic requirement, and access was needed to the outbuildings. A hot tub close to the house was also wanted – an unusual feature in a suburban garden, but common in Eastern cultures. The tub is connected to the domestic water and heating supplies and incorporates a pump and water filter.

With any long, narrow garden one of the main tasks is to create a feeling of space and movement, leading the eye away from the boundaries and breaking the space down into more manageable sections. As the rear of the house is in shade for much of the day, it made sense to site the main sitting area where it would catch the sun at the far end of the garden, adjoining the outbuildings. The sitting area is linked to the house by a series of walkways.

The space is nearly three times as long as it is wide, so the area was organized into a corresponding number of 'rooms', with each section roughly similar in size to detract from the overall length.

Timber decking

The first and most important of the outdoor rooms is the timber-decked sitting area and pool. Timber is traditional in Oriental gardens and makes superb flooring. It has been used with great flair to form a stylish framework set at different angles and levels to make the most of a fairly restricted space.

For timber decking to wear well and look good in Britain's damp and temperate climate, careful planning and sound construction techniques are essential. There must be adequate ventilation beneath the deck, and stout floor joists, suitably treated with an appropriate preservative – avoid creosote which is poisonous to plants – should be bolted to posts set into concrete.

▶ **Wood and water** Natural elements are all important in traditional Japanese gardens, with a hint of mystery. Apparently simplistic, the garden is the result of the endless attention to detail that creates harmony.

The type of timber used for decking can vary: softwood if pressure treated is suitable; a hardwood such as Western red cedar or one of the African timbers (iroko or teak) gives an extended life but at a higher initial cost.

The boards in the decking are set at an angle to lead feet and eyes on a diagonal axis across the garden. Diagonal lines are the longest length across a rectangle and therefore give a feeling of increased space. The angled walkways create interesting diversions, and are far more effective than a path leading straight up and down the garden.

While the decked floor has been stained a dark brown, the boundaries are covered with light-coloured woven rush screen panels – an admirable way to hide unsightly surfaces in such a setting, and the perfect foil for planting. Rush matting also covers the outside of the shed, merging it into the overall composition and increasing the illusion of a Far Eastern environment.

The timber-decked sitting area beneath the wooden pergola is set square with the boundaries, forming a more conventional, static space across the width of the garden, with the deck dropping down in a single broad step to the surround of the pool.

Water features

A pool is obligatory in such a setting. This calm stretch of water not only creates reflections from sky and poolside planting but also subdivides the terrace from the softer parts of the garden that lead back towards the house.

The black butyl rubber liner used for the pool gives an impression of depth and mystery. A liner works well here, being easily tucked up under the decking on three sides and into a beach of loose pebbles on the other.

To reinforce the Oriental theme, koi carp swim in the pool. The colours of these fish vary enormously, from gold to black and white. They grow large in time – and tame enough to be fed by hand – so a generous sheet of water like this is perfect.

Excavated soil from the pool was used to create a rockery, and the liner was extended to make a stream bed that flows back into the pool – power is provided by a submersible pump. The sound of gently lapping water can be heard throughout the garden.

A timber bridge spans the water, the plain bamboo handrail echoing the natural material used in the boundary screen. A particular strength of this garden is the way soft and hard features complement each other. For example,

The irregularly-shaped pool is lined with tough black butyl and stocked with reeds, water lilies and koi carp. Open to the sky, the decking surround is wide enough for sunbathing and relaxation

Timber decking is set at different angles and levels to make interesting walkways through the garden. It needs annual scrubbing down to remove dangerous and slippery algae

N

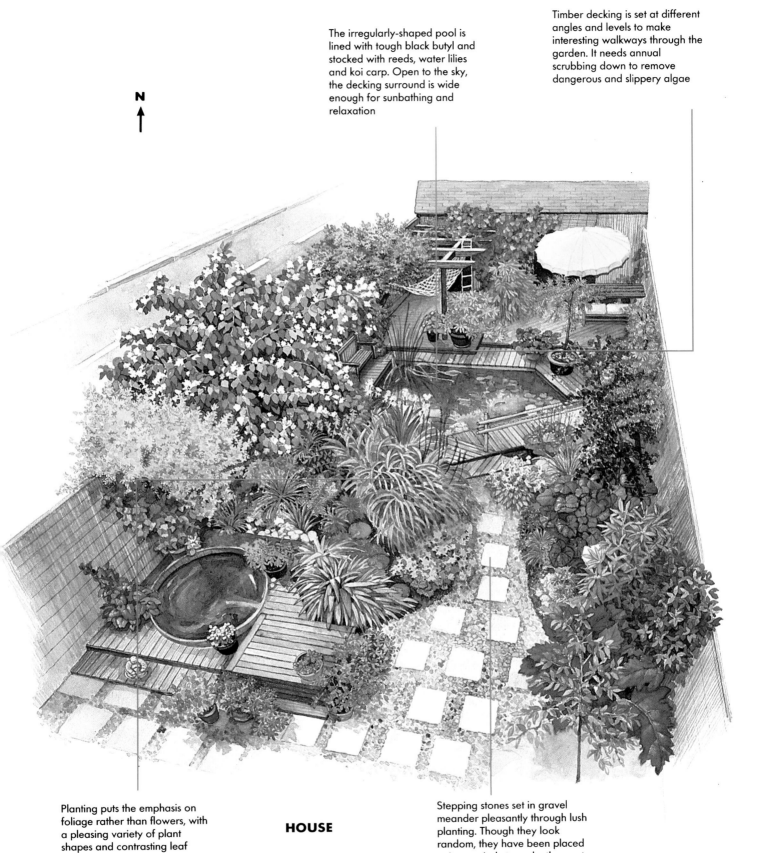

Planting puts the emphasis on foliage rather than flowers, with a pleasing variety of plant shapes and contrasting leaf forms. Plants in pots add extra flexibility to a small garden since they can be moved about to create different effects

HOUSE

Stepping stones set in gravel meander pleasantly through lush planting. Though they look random, they have been placed quite precisely to make the most of a small space as the path narrows from an open space to a single-line through lush foliage that partly obscures the rest of the garden

◄ **Timber decking** The raised wooden patio extends to the pool surround crossed by a bridge from which to contemplate the still water. A black pool liner gives an illusion of depth and reflects the open sky above.

► **Moisture lovers** Marginal plants by the pool edge include golden-flowered giant king cup (*Caltha polypetala*) and the plantain-like *Alisma plantiago* with dainty white flower sprays. The massive leaf clumps contrast charmingly with the feathery foliage of mountain ash by the rush-covered fence.

▼ **Mirror images** A still sheet of water is disturbed only by colourful koi carp darting among clumps of water reeds and breaking the reflection of sky and overhead trees.

Planting

This is essentially a plant-lover's garden and the trees are particularly delightful.

The purple-leaved birch (*Betula pendula* 'Purpurea') is a slow-growing rather delicate tree that requires a sheltered environment. The birch makes a handsome contrast to the rich green of giant king cup (*Caltha polypetala*) at the pool margin and golden privet.

Another well-chosen tree with an elegant spreading habit is mountain ash (*Sorbus vilmorinii*). The fern-like foliage is superb in autumn when it turns purple and red, and the fruit is attractive too, borne in loose drooping clusters that change colour with age from deep pink to almost white. In time, the tree branches will droop gracefully over the bridge. A decidedly Oriental choice was the Chinese cherry, *Prunus* 'Shirofugen', with flowers that open white and fade to a delicate pale purple among young copper-coloured leaves.

The shrubs are a mixture of deciduous and evergreen species, with fatsia and privet making a bold show in winter. Of the bamboos, *Arundinaria japonica* is particularly fine. The leaf margins of another bamboo, *Sasa palmata*, can die off in winter, giving it at first glance an attractive variegation. It's a fairly rampant bamboo, and needs to be kept in check. The grass *Miscanthus sacchariflorus* is also vigorous, reaching 2m (6ft 6ins) in a relatively short time.

Planting at a lower level concentrates on hardy perennials that thrive in the moist soil by the waterside – there's a fine selection of hostas, *Ligularia, Caltha, Trollius* and *Rodgersia*.

Two specimens of pyracantha and yucca were saved from the original planting; both provided welcome greenery while the new plants were becoming established, and now make fine evergreen accent plants.

Pots are a versatile feature in the garden – and reminiscent of the East – as portable containers for instant colour in the form of spring bulbs and summer annuals and for more permanent plantings, too. Container plants include *Fatsia japonica* with its large leaves and the delightful *Caragana arborescens* which has pea-like flowers in late spring.

The pots themselves are chosen to be complementary to particular

the bridge is aligned to focus on a fine yucca, one of the few plants retained from the original garden.

Paths and paving

The bridge marks a transition in the garden, leading from the essentially hard landscape of the timber deck, pergola and pool through to the softer planted area negotiated by stepping stones. The plants form a tension point, with two wings of foliage almost closing together and heightening the change of mood.

The stepping stones are laid with great skill – the loose cobbles are a perfect foil to crisp paving slabs and plants. Apparently laid at random, they perform a precise function, linking the exit from the house to the far-end patio in a meandering line that increases the sense of spaciousness, and of mystery where the path narrows through lush vegetation.

Near the house the informality of random steps gives way to carefully laid slabs in straight lines

that lead across to the hot tub. As elsewhere in the garden, the attention to detail is complete: the cobbles are set in mortar and laid tightly together to give a sense of natural order in the area beside the house.

The hot tub itself is neatly screened from the rest of the garden, wrapped around in soft foliage. It is partly sunk into the decking, with a raised platform to give access to the tub, and sheltered by rush matting. Heating comes from the domestic supply, and the tub is covered over when not in use.

In the dining area, tables and chairs have been chosen to blend with the decking and overhead beams. This is the ultimate outdoor room, used extensively for entertaining and relaxation.

In a garden that relies heavily on the texture and juxtaposition of foliage rather than flowers, a yellow parasol perfectly picks up the colour of golden privet and the majestic spires of *Ligularia*.

plants. Though many of them are Oriental, the rest are a pleasantly varied mix that has been collected over the years.

Overall, the hard and soft landscape elements in this garden are in perfect harmony, with a juxtaposition of natural and manufactured features supporting one another to produce a delightful outside room.

The garden is easy to care for; the only real work is maintenance of the decking and gentle disciplining of some of the more vigorous planting which, left unchecked, could eventually upset the fine balance.

▶ **Contrasting leaf textures** Foliage plants dominate in Oriental gardens. A giant *Miscanthus*, its grassy leaves trembling in the breeze, contrasts in colour, shape and texture with the rigid, spine-tipped leaf blades of yucca.

▼ **Hot tub** Endemic to Japanese culture is the outdoor hot tub — the equivalent of the Scandinavian sauna — in which to relax in natural surroundings.

MEDITERRANEAN GARDENS

White walls, terracotta pots, gravel and an abundance of sun-loving plants give this formal garden a strong Mediterranean feel.

This gravel garden is surrounded on all four sides by high walls. They have been whitewashed and are topped with terracotta tiles which instantly create a Mediterranean atmosphere.

The garden is a sun-trap – a factor used to good effect in the choice of drought-tolerant and grey-leaved plants, both of which contribute to the 'hot' feel of the garden. A thick layer of light-coloured gravel makes an easy-care surface.

Originally, the site was sloping, with a 1m (3ft) drop across the width of the garden. The soil is sticky and strongly alkaline, and becomes rock hard in summer. In winter it is heavy, though not waterlogged. The south-facing site is sunny, and the pale walls reflect heat as well as providing shelter from harsh winds, making it a perfect spot for tender plants.

The layout
The design, roughly cross-shaped in plan, is based on rectangles and squares. An ornamental cherry tree (*Prunus* sp), growing in a central position at the junction of four wide gravel paths, became the pivot of the layout, creating a pleasing asymmetry.

Raised beds not only provide the free drainage that sun-loving alpine and grey-leaved plants need, but also the opportunity to create a formal, geometric pattern in three dimensions. The use of railway sleepers, an easy and relatively inexpensive way to build retaining walls if you can get hold of them, reinforces the linear, angular quality of the design. Although not part of the original plan, one of the raised beds running along the length of a boundary wall is used as a nursery and for propagation.

A pergola along one wall creates a shady walkway, provides support for climbing roses, and helps conceal less than perfect views out. Running parallel to the north-facing boundary wall, the pergola is a free-standing structure so that light and air can circulate freely among the climbing plants, thus reducing the incidence of disease.

Access and an attractive view into the garden from a courtyard are gained via an archway in a newly built, white-washed wall. A second archway, framed by vigorous wall shrubs, leads into another section, a well-tended kitchen garden.

▼ **Mediterranean flavour** White-washed walls surround this sun-filled garden lavishly stocked with foliage and flowering plants, which tumble over the edges of raised beds. A mature cherry tree casts dappled shade.

A collection of stone troughs and sink gardens, some genuine stone, others glazed and dressed with a mixture of adhesive and cement to imitate weathered stone, make a distinctive feature in one corner. They display sun-loving alpines, predominantly summer-flowering houseleeks (*Sempervivum* spp), many of which are grown individually in shallow, terracotta half-pots.

Small groupings of stone boulders imitate a miniature mountainside. Of sculptural interest, they contrast in scale with the gravel and in form with the raised rectangular planting beds. Along the south-facing paved sitting area is a larger alpine meadow, complete with rocks and stone chippings and home to several clumps of brightly coloured alpines and dwarf shrubs.

At the end of the rockery, a low wooden seat gives views across the entire garden and catches the evening sun.

Construction materials

The sloping site was levelled by cutting and filling, with a small amount of excavated soil moved to another plot. The fourth wall, which completes the enclosure, was built of concrete breeze blocks, but rendered and tiled to tone in with the existing walls.

One large tree, a sugar maple (*Acer saccharum*), was removed from the back of the site to maximize the available sunlight, but the flowering cherry remained as the garden's main focal point.

The raised beds are made of railway sleepers, bought in large quantities from a sleeper contractor. Wherever cut, the exposed wood was treated with preservative. The retaining walls are two or three sleepers high and laid on a foundation of short lengths of sawn-off sleepers. The lowest sleepers are set slightly below the ground level surface, to prevent debris filling the cavities and for appearance's sake.

The pergola is made of treated larch poles. Again, any cut sections were re-treated. The poles were sunk straight into the ground, and show no signs of rot. Concrete foundations for wooden poles sometimes cause, rather than prevent, rot as water can become trapped in the tiny space between the pole and the concrete.

A mature cherry tree acts as the central focal point. Clean, angular lines provided by long lengths of railway sleeper add a formal touch to the design. Raised beds aid drainage — vital for sun-loving Mediterranean plants. Extensive areas of gravel add to the atmosphere

Topped by red tiles, an archway breaks the expanse of white-washed wall. Pink and white climbing roses frame the opening and tall foxgloves (*Digitalis purpurea*) add height to the planting. A tree peony thrives in the sheltered position

Stone troughs and terracotta bowls enhance the garden's Mediterranean aura. Planted with a variety of houseleeks, they provide evergreen interest and, in summer, pink flowers. Grouped together, large limestone boulders create a natural ornamental feature

N

A rustic pergola, covered with climbing roses, runs along one boundary. Providing pleasant shade, it ends with a simple focal point – a terrracotta forcing jar. The path consists of railway sleepers, their edges hidden by thickly planted London pride (*Saxifraga umbrosa*)

A nursery bed occupies one raised border along a sunny, sheltered boundary wall. Shrubs including a tree daisy (*Olearia* sp) break up the nursery rows of young plants and the wall is covered with *Clematis montana* and *Clematis orientalis*

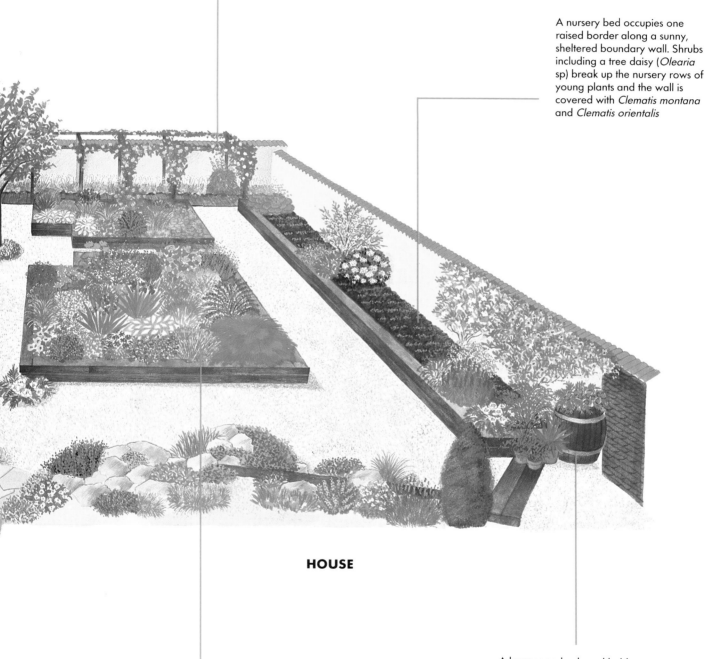

HOUSE

Raised beds are filled with a variety of perennials, alpines, bulbs and low shrubs. Around the edges, ground cover is provided by many summer-flowering plants, such as bellflowers (*Campanula carpatica*). Height accents come from ornamental grasses

A large wooden barrel holds a bush tomato as a backdrop to a collection of terracotta pots planted with colourful fuchsias and variegated New Zealand flax (*Phormium tenax*). The composition is balanced by a conical Lawson's cypress (*Chamaecyparis lawsoniana* 'Ellwoodii')

Under the pergola runs a railway sleeper path, half a sleeper wide, bedded on sand.

Gravel is readily available from builder's merchants, garden centres and DIY stores, and is a cheap, attractive alternative to more expensive forms of paving. The whole area was first treated with a weedkiller, then given a foundation of crushed hardcore. A 10cm (4in) layer of gravel was topped with a finishing layer, 2.5cm (1in) thick, of shingle which is regularly raked level. The large, ornamental stone boulders are limestone.

Planting schemes

This is essentially a plantsman's garden and plants take pride of place over any ornaments. The choice of plants is dictated by the sheltered, sunny position and the free-draining, lime-rich soil.

It is very much a summer garden, early summer in particular, when the majority of alpine plants come into bloom. At other times of the year, colour comes from winter and spring-flowering bulbs, such as winter-flowering irises, crocuses and species tulips, and the lush growth of several ornamental

grasses. Facing the garden from the courtyard arch, colours range from stronger, richer ones on the left of the path, to paler, softer ones on the right.

The garden includes old-fashioned and modern shrub roses, and mixed climbers along the walls. Some are fragrant, but all are soft coloured. The climbers, which help to break up the large area of wall, include white-

▲ **Evergreen houseleeks** A collection of half-pots holds a large range of sempervivums, displaying a variety of forms and colours against a weathered stone trough 'planted' with large limestone rocks.

▼ **Planting beds** Raised beds constructed from railway sleepers improve the sharp drainage essential for most alpines. Flower colours are soft and muted among strong foliage that runs from dark green to silvery-grey.

▶ **Terracotta pink** A tile-topped archway gives glimpses into the walled kitchen garden. Climbing roses clothe the walls, and at ground level alpine pots and washed shingle repeat the colour scheme of the wall.

flowered summer jasmine (*Jasminum officinale*), *Clematis montana* and *Clematis orientalis*.

Along the southern boundary wall London pride (*Saxifraga umbrosa*) dominates the planting under the pergola. The plants, taking advantage of the lightly shaded site, produce dainty sprays of pink flowers long into late spring. The pergola itself supports climbing roses; at one end, a large forcing jar adds a charming rustic touch, its terracotta colour adding warmth to the dark evergreen foliage of a *Stranvaesia davidiana*. This turns crimson in autumn, complementing the drooping clusters of red berries that follow the white early-summer flowers.

The raised beds are densely planted with a wide variety of sun-loving plants that thrive in the free-draining soil. Low-growing plants are concentrated around the edges of the beds and include tussock bell-flowers (*Campanula carpatica*), Jacob's ladder (*Polemonium carneum*) and Mexican poppy (*Argemone mexicana*) which produces orange or red flowers.

Central accents are formed by taller plants, such as New Zealand flax (*Phormium tenax*) and several pines (*Pinus nigra*) that reinforce the garden's continental flavour. Foxgloves (*Digitalis purpurea*) echo the vertical lines of the eastern archway.

Maintenance

This unusual type of garden requires a maintenance regime similar to that of other gardens with one or two exceptions. The beds need weeding, but weeds in the thick layer of gravel are rarely troublesome. Cultivated plants and some wild plants, such as foxglove, that self-sow in the gravel become part of the garden scene.

▶ **Pergola walk** Sweetly scented roses clamber over a framework of larch poles, swathes of pink-flowered London pride at their feet. At the end of the vista, a large bell-shaped forcing jar appears superimposed on the wall.

▲ **Mediterranean plants** Trees and shrubs native to the mountains of southern Europe revel in the sunny enclosed garden. From the archway a black pine (*Pinus nigra*) surveys clumps of sprawling bright-coloured rock roses (*Cistus* sp).

▶ **Barrel tomatoes** A trailing bush tomato spills over pots of hardy fuchsias. On the wall above, a vigorous *Clematis orientalis* spreads open its yellow-purple sepals, thick-skinned like orange peel.

Watering is done regularly in hot, dry weather because raised beds dry out quickly. Plants growing in sinks and alpine pans and in the rockery are largely drought-resistant.

The sheltered environment protects a number of half-hardy plants. They are given no special winter protection, but cuttings are taken from the risky or definitely tender ones, such as black horehound (*Ballota pseudodictamnus*) and twinspur (*Diascia barberae*). The cuttings are kept in a cool greenhouse over winter and planted out the following spring.

This Mediterranean-style garden was neither difficult nor time-consuming to create. Many of the plants are readily available from local nurseries.

TOPIARY FRAMEWORK

**Topiary adds elegance and form
to modest as well as grand gardens, with
free-standing sculptures as focal points.**

Though often associated with vast schemes on grand estates, topiary also applies to such small examples as a standard clipped bay tree on a balcony or terrace, and there are many options in between to suit most schemes.

Topiary is easy to include in any garden, and it can be adapted to almost any layout, either as a major feature or used as isolated focal points.

Being woody and usually evergreen, topiary is a valuable partner for short-term flowers – annuals, biennials, bulbs, perennials and herbs. In season, these plants display their foliage and flowers against the formal lines of topiary. In winter the topiary performs a holding exercise, focusing the eye when herbaceous plants are dormant.

Formal clipped hedges can provide boundaries, backdrops, screens, internal walls or edging, according to location and height. An existing hedge can be made more decorative if pruned to form crenellations or finials along the top. Free-standing topiary sculptures can provide focal points or – used in pairs or rows – set up pleasing rhythms.

A topiary corridor
The garden shown here combines topiary hedging and free-standing sculptures. It is a section of a larger garden, but the layout could easily be self-contained. And with a little adjustment, the design could suit gardens of different proportions, and individual sections could provide inspiration for small areas of ground.

Long, narrow plots are sometimes considered awkward, but this thin strip of land has been transformed into a splendid topiary garden, filled in with herbs. The simple symmetrical plan reflects the formality of the topiary, and is based on interlinked rectangles and circles.

The layout consists of a narrow central gravel path edged in brick, with an old millstone surrounded

---

▼ **Green corridor** A long narrow plot has been transformed into a sunny corridor of closely clipped yew hedges formalized with curves and rounded finials. Free-standing box spirals stand sentinel in the corners, and rounded domes of golden box accentuate borders of cottage-garden herbs.

Brick-edged gravel paths and an open centre reinforce the design.

A box spiral stands like a sentinel in each corner of the garden. Four such free-standing sculptures, each corkscrewing out of the ground, guard the entrance and exit

by a wide gravel circle at the half-way point. This widening out of the central area creates a feeling of generous space in spite of the narrowness of the plot.

Bordering the path and central circle are narrow beds, accessible for maintenance. At one end, flag-stone paving at right angles to the path forms a T-shaped seating area.

Framework planting

Tall, clipped yew hedges enclose the garden, providing shelter and privacy. At the far end, the hedge is lower, clipped into curves and with a gap that affords views beyond the garden. The curves end in clipped ball-shaped finials, marking the entrance to the topi-ary garden.

The ball theme is repeated in three pairs of clipped ball-shaped

▲ **Foliage contrasts** Golden box shaped into well-rounded spheres punctuates the edges of the central circle. Bright green mint, its roots constrained in a terracotta pot, repeats the circular theme, the tall graceful leaf fronds and yellow flower clusters of fennel towering above.

shrubs of golden box placed at regular intervals along the path.

Four tall spiral-trained box trees are planted symmetrically, one in each corner of the garden, to contrast with the golden ball shapes and with the informal, sprawling herbs surrounding them.

The topiary sculptures are all carefully tended and in excellent condition. A disadvantage of topi-ary – particularly where a shape is repeated – is that any flaws quickly become obvious.

Handsome containers reinforce the circular elements in the garden. The terracotta pots are more than decorative — they contain herbs that would be too invasive in the border

Walls of evergreen yew enclose the narrow plot to give shelter and seclusion. The ends are clipped into curves and topped with ball-shaped finials to create an elegant vista

The centrepiece of the garden is an old millstone set in a circle of gravel with a brick surround. Circular elements draw the attention away from what could be an awkward corridor shape

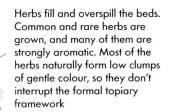

Herbs fill and overspill the beds. Common and rare herbs are grown, and many of them are strongly aromatic. Most of the herbs naturally form low clumps of gentle colour, so they don't interrupt the formal topiary framework

Clipped topiary spheres punctuate the path and emphasize the millstone focal point. Golden box is an excellent contrast to the darker green of the other topiary features

Paving by the entrance is brick-edged stone which leads on to the wide gravel path. The hard materials are mellow in colour, and softened by plants spilling from borders and pots

Yew, box and privet are the most suitable plants to achieve the precision needed for general topiary work, as they are small leaved, evergreen and respond well to pruning. Hornbeam or beech could be substituted for the yew hedge; they are faster growing but provide no winter greenery – though both retain attractive rich brown leaves through winter.

Tall bay trees trained into a flame shape, or naturally erect-growing Irish yews or Irish junipers, would give roughly the same effect as the spiral topiary, but without their precision. And there are many dwarf thujas and false cypresses with naturally round growth habits that could be used instead of the clipped, ball-shaped box in this garden.

Herb infills

With the exception of mazes, few gardens are based entirely on topiary – a blend of topiary and non-topiary plants in fact enhances both types of plant. In this sunny site with well-drained soil, medicinal, culinary and cosmetic herbs fill and overspill the borders in a range of green, gold, silver, purple and grey foliage in plain and variegated forms.

For a garden on a smaller scale, the choice could be confined to the more useful culinary herbs, with perhaps a special exception made for lavender. The more invasive herbs, such as mint and lemon balm, are best contained in pots.

Popular kitchen and ornamental herbs grown here include fennel, thyme, rosemary, sage, chives, garlic, tarragon, mint, marjoram and lavender. More unusual herbs are grown, too, such as sorrel, wormwood, aniseed, angelica, hyssop, coriander, borage, woodruff and burnet.

In addition to the open-grown herbs, there are herb-filled terracotta pots, strategically placed in the central circle to reinforce the symmetry.

Even in high season, herbs produce modest flowers and gentle rather than vibrant colour: the yellows of silver-leaved daisy-family herbs such as artemisias, the mauves of lavender and mints, and the greeny whites and yellows of umbellifers such as angelica. Most of these herbs are excellent for attracting butterflies and bees.

For a more colourful show of flowers, which would work equally well within a topiary framework, a mixture of annuals, herbaceous perennials and bulbs could be substituted.

Both herb and herbaceous gardens are labour intensive, involving weeding, lifting and dividing, and possibly staking and replacing. To cut down the work load without loss of colour, the beds could be filled with low-growing shrubs and ground-cover plants.

Tall plants should be avoided since they would interrupt the clean, geometric lines of the topiary, and possibly make the task of clipping the hedges awkward.

A third more subtle arrangement would be to replace the ornamental plants with a grass or chamomile lawn. Dwarf box could then edge the path, emphasizing the architectural quality of the design. Such edging blends well with formal or informal schemes.

▲ **Topiary shapes** Symmetrical spirals can be created by twisting the main stem of a supple young box – or yew – round a stake, but it will take several years to achieve the desired effect. For quicker results, cheat slightly by choosing a more mature plant and clipping it to shape.

Mark out a wide spiral shape with two lengths of string and carefully clip the foliage away right to the main stem. Maintain the shape with trimming at least once a year.

▶ **Yew walls** Close clipped yew hedges enclose a scene of seclusion and quiet contemplation. Circular themes add variety of form – spiralling green box, spheres of golden box and rounded yew finials by the entrance.

An old millstone set within a gravel circle widens the perspective, and on the paved sitting area, a miniature stone pool marvellously mirrors the scudding clouds above.

◄ **Box spheres** Rows of green box trimmed to perfect rounds follow the lines of a long rose pergola, and ribbons of dwarf box edge the path beneath.

Such topiary features can easily be adapted to suit gardens of more modest size. The shapes are easily maintained and will continue to provide interest long after the roses have passed their glorious prime.

▼ **Topiary duck** Fashioned from golden privet, a duck sculpture strikes a light-hearted note. Animal and bird shapes demand both skill and patience – galvanized wire forms make the task easier and can be obtained from specialist shops. Start with simple geometric shapes – cubes, spheres and pyramids – before you progress to more complex forms.

Topiary shapes

In topiary, plants are treated like clay – raw material to be formed into a wide variety of shapes. As with clay, some topiary shapes – such as spheres, angular cubes, cones and pyramids, or simple forms of edging – are easier to execute than others. These tend to be the most popular forms of topiary, and are ideal for the beginner to start work on.

Ribbons of dwarf shrubs such as box, planted single file or in tightly staggered rows, can follow almost any curve or series of straight lines and angles. A dwarf box edging can make right angles with great precision.

Ribbon edging can be square in section, tapered towards the top, or rounded. An edging prevents border plants spilling over lawn edge or paving, while allowing light to reach them and their beauty to be seen.

Edging on either side of a path – especially where the path runs through flower borders – is traditional in formal garden layouts, and often very handsome.

Spheres, also called globes or balls, are pleasing to the eye from every direction. They can be free-

standing or grown as finials topping formal hedges.

Topiary spheres can be any size, though miniature spheres look best in containers – otherwise they may disappear into the general garden mêlée.

Pairs or rows of spheres can repeat the rhythm set up by nearby features, such as pergolas, or create a rhythm of their own. If the same topiary shape is repeated each plant must look healthy and as similar as possible to the others. Misshapen or under-sized specimens stand out like missing teeth.

Arches in topiary are especially impressive and can be trained over free-standing metal framework or as a continuation of a hedge. Arches are long-term projects, since a height of about 1.8m (6ft) must be reached before the final shaping takes place.

Animals form the whimsical side of topiary, and range from friendly little birds to elegant peacocks or strange mythological beasts.

Animals are the hardest shapes to form – it's difficult to make them look realistic, even when trained over galvanized wire forms.

JAPANESE GARDENS

**The essence of a Japanese garden captures
nature itself, in its use of stones, water and
colourful trees and shrubs.**

The heart of the suburbs may seem an unpromising location for an authentic Japanese garden, but this example shows what can be achieved in just such a setting. Although the owner works in the horticultural trade, he had no specialist knowledge of Japanese gardening when he began. His main asset was enthusiasm, and he built up the garden over many years, learning as he went along.

Japanese gardens are usually designed to be viewed from the house, with secondary views from pavilions, bridges or special viewing stones.

The site
The plot is a self-contained, rectangular back garden, approximately 18 × 12m (60 × 40ft), on a typical suburban housing estate. It was originally laid to lawn, with straight herbaceous borders round the sides, and a small rockery, which has since been enlarged.

The south-facing garden is fairly sheltered. Additional shelter is provided by woven bamboo panels, 1.8m (6ft) high, attached to conventional perimeter fencing. The soil is neutral and reasonably moisture-retentive.

Planning and development
Unlike many garden layouts, which start from an overall master plan, this garden developed gradually from a single Japanese feature. The starting point was a group of three shrubs: a Japanese maple (*Acer palmatum* 'Dissectum'); *Pieris japonica* 'Variegata', an attractive silver-variegated evergreen shrub; and a dwarf Hinoki cypress (*Chamaecyparis obtusa* 'Nana').

The owner was unaware of their shared Oriental origins, but found the combination of their forms and foliage pleasing.

▶ **Stone lanterns** Originally used in shrines and temples for holding votive offerings, lanterns of various shapes and sizes light up meandering stepping stone paths. Tradition dictates plants of Japanese origin.

Soon afterwards, at a visit to the famous Japanese Garden of Compton Acres, near Bournemouth, a Buddha statue was acquired and with that the inspiration to enlarge upon the Japanese theme. Since then, more Oriental plants and features have been added over the years.

Philosophy and design
Every feature in a Japanese garden is symbolic of something else, whether a concept, such as long life, or an element of nature, such as a mountain. Often a single feature will be symbolic of several ideas, on different levels. Rocks and water are of great importance.

Miniaturization plays a crucial part in Japanese gardens, in which many features must be contained within a small space. Formality and ritualized tradition are also important, so that all classical Japanese gardens share the same common visual 'language'.

This garden may be divided roughly into five sections, each following a different Japanese style. There is a shrine garden, a tea garden, and a dry-landscape or Zen garden. A hill garden makes a pleasant backdrop, while a central lawn area represents a Japanese 'flat' garden.

Garden components
The most dramatic feature is the scaled-down dry-landscape or Zen garden, near the miniature tea house and reached through a

The dry stream is a distinctive Japanese feature. Pebbles fill a former artificial stream, arranged to simulate the flow of water. Fine gravel or marble chips can also be used, and tiny pieces of slate, bedded in sand in mosaic patterns, will create the impression of moving water

Stepping stones in the 'flat garden' are laid in curving irregular lines, in keeping with Japanese tradition. Occasional large rocks are set among the smaller ones, as reminders of stone's endurance in a changing world. Some stepping stones are decorated with graphic symbols – four depict the seasons of the year

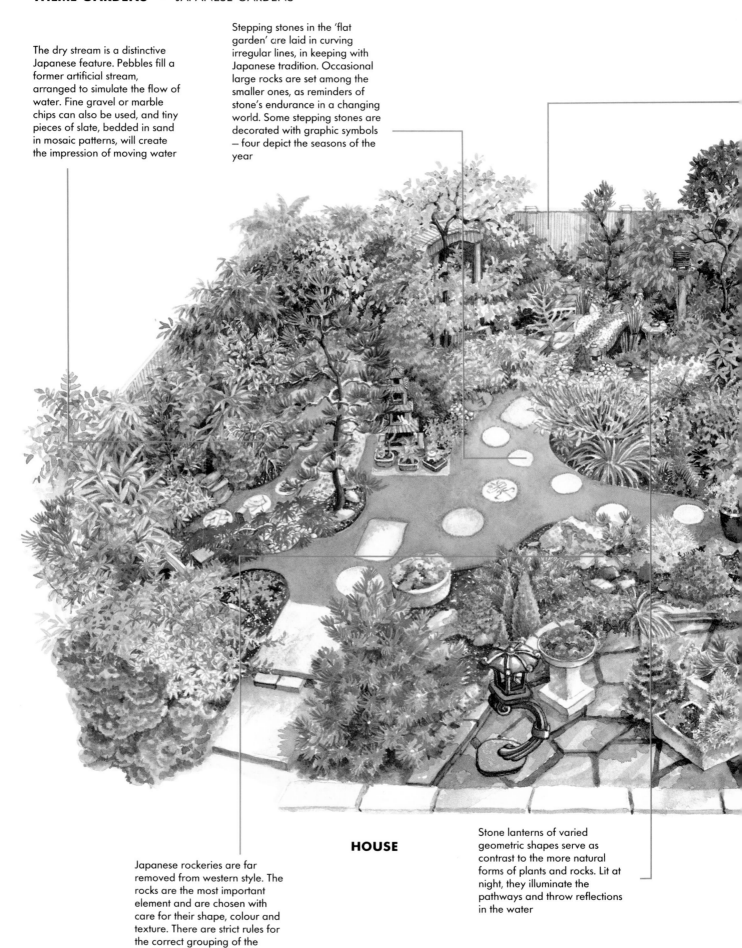

HOUSE

Japanese rockeries are far removed from western style. The rocks are the most important element and are chosen with care for their shape, colour and texture. There are strict rules for the correct grouping of the stones, which often represent particular concepts

Stone lanterns of varied geometric shapes serve as contrast to the more natural forms of plants and rocks. Lit at night, they illuminate the pathways and throw reflections in the water

Woven bamboo panels, 1.8m (6ft) high, are attached to the boundary fencing, and provide additional shelter. A dry-landscape or Zen garden and miniature tea house are concealed behind mature trees and shrubs

N

The 'well' is operated by concealed pipes. Water drips continually from a bucket suspended above a stone sink and splashes softly into the basin below. Water is symbolic of life and associated with purification

bamboo gate. The rocks set in the gravel may represent mountains, according to tradition, or perhaps islands in the sea, depending on their shape.

The tea house is built of square-mesh wooden garden trellis. Tea houses are classed according to the number of floor mats they contain – this is a 'four-and-a-half mat' tea house.

The garden has three pools, the longest of which features a waterfall. In Japanese gardening, water is an essential element, sometimes symbolically so as in Zen gardens, but more often as actual streams and pools. Always referred to as a lake or sea, a pool, however small, is irregular in shape, and a stream should wind along naturally, sometimes splashing over a waterfall. The banks may be shored up with rocks or low-growing plants or they may merge into a stretch of pebble-strewn beach.

All the pools are serviced by circulating pumps, one operating a traditional 'deer scarer'. This is a

bamboo pipe set on a pivot, which creates a regular, soft plonking sound. Another pump operates a water basin, for washing before partaking in the tea ceremony.

Three bridges can be found in the garden. One is a traditional stone half-moon bridge, another a simple stone slab, with end stones on either side. The third consists of two stones, with a gap between them, through which evil spirits will fall, according to folklore.

One very striking stone feature is the result of a happy accident. An artificial stream, made of flexible polythene covered with a layer of stones, sprang a leak at the height of the 'Open Garden' season, when hundreds of visitors were expected.

Since there was no time for repairs, the stones were quickly rearranged to represent the tum-

▼ **Japanese garden design** The object of a true Japanese garden is to create a space of peace and quiet in which to contemplate nature and restore inner harmony.

THE ZEN GARDEN

▲ The entrance is through a bamboo gate, partly concealed by shrubs.

► The purest and highest form of Japanese gardening is the dry-landscape or Zen garden. This type of garden is meant to be contemplated, not trodden — it demands a response to the beauty of abstract shape. In most Zen gardens, rocks are arranged as mountains in a symbolic sea of fine gravel, which is raked into different patterns every day, following strict tradition.

bling flow of water. This feature proved popular and has been allowed to remain.

In keeping with the Japanese tradition, the stepping stones in the 'flat garden' are not laid in straight lines, and occasional large stones are set among the smaller ones, so that visitors can stop to rest or view the garden.

Some of the stepping stones are decorated with graphic symbols: for instance, four of them represent the seasons of the year. The stone symbolizing spring is the farthest from the house, as spring is traditionally the most longed-for season.

Stone lanterns containing candles light up the pathways at night. The formal geometric shapes of the lanterns also serve as contrast to the more natural forms of plants and rocks.

A recent feature is a 'well' made from a waterproofed, old stone sink placed slightly above ground level. On top of this is a woven bamboo lid, with a bucket suspended above. Concealed pipes and a circulating pump help to create the illusion that the bucket has just been drawn from the 'well' – water drips continually from the brim of the bucket to the bamboo lid and into the basin below, making a pleasant soft sound.

Planting

Japanese plants usually thrive in temperate gardens, provided the soil and aspect are suitable.

Bamboos and rhododendrons, Japanese maples, Japanese ferns, conifers and water plants make up the basic planting structure of this garden. Among the maples are *Acer palmatum* 'Dissectum Atropurpureum', with deep purple leaves; *A. japonicum* 'Aureum', with soft yellow leaves; and *A. palmatum* 'Osakazuki', with green leaves turning fiery scarlet in autumn.

The bamboos include *Arundinaria variegata*, which forms low dense thickets of pale green canes; *A. murielae*, an elegant species with bright green canes, maturing to a dull yellow-green; and *A. viridi-striata*, a variegated bamboo, with purplish-green canes and narrow dark green leaves, heavily striped yellow.

The only Western plant in the garden is the corkscrew hazel (*Corylus avellana* 'Contorta'). This British shrub is, however, quite Oriental in appearance.

Flower power

Although many of the brashest flowering cherries, azaleas, rhododendrons and camellias have Oriental origins, flowers play a secondary role in traditional Japanese gardens: form and foliage are all-important.

Some compromises can be made, and Japanese clematis, Japanese rhododendrons, Japanese roses, and autumn-flowering Japanese camellias are all encouraged to bloom in this garden. Most dra-

▲ **Stone basin** An essential part of the ancient tea ceremony, a hollowed-out stone stands by the entrance to the tea house. A bamboo water dipper rests traditionally across it.

matic of all are the Japanese wisterias with their 1m (3ft) long flower racemes – the lilac-flowered, fragrant *Wisteria floribunda* 'Macrobotrys', and a white-flowered cultivar ('Alba').

Seasonal impact
For late autumn, winter and early spring interest, well over half the plants are evergreen. From mid spring onwards, the fresh colours of young deciduous leaves unfurling are a major feature, together with cherry blossom and the orange-red blooms of the deciduous *Rhododendron japonicum*.

The Japanese maples turn brilliant colours in autumn – yellow, orange, bronze and red – partnered by the bright orange seed pods of Chinese lanterns (*Physalis alkekengi*).

An unusual early winter-flowering camellia, *Camellia sasanqua* 'Variegata', bears small, and scented pink-flushed white flowers as well as grey-green leaves, margined white.

One unusual seasonal feature is a container which holds the traditional 'plant of the month'. In October, for example, a chrysanthemum takes pride of place; in January a dwarf Japanese white pine, *Pinus parviflora*; and in February, a flowering plum.

Maintenance
The garden has quite specific requirements for maintenance. Nearly all the plants in the garden are shrubs, trees or perennials, so there is no need for transplanting or bedding out. A small green-

▲ **Dragon-eye pine** A young *Pinus densiflora* 'Oculus-draconis' unites the enduring elements of water and stone. In the foreground is a Japanese cedar (*Cryptomeria japonica*).

▼ **Half-moon bridge** Spanning a dry-stream bed, a traditional stone bridge is almost concealed by a clump of variegated bamboos and the colourful foliage of Japanese maples.

▲ **Stone Buddha** Close to the statue is the container that holds the 'plant of the month', to represent both the unchanging and the transient.

▼ **Traditional elements** Trees, especially conifers, shrubs and ground cover, are more important than short-term flowers in a Japanese garden.

house provides the minimal winter shelter needed for the hardy bonsai trees.

In Japanese terms, the garden is overplanted, so a fair amount of pruning and thinning is needed. Bamboos are cut back hard in winter. To keep the plants small, they receive no fertilizer of any sort.

The main pool is netted in the autumn, to keep out the leaves and protect the valuable koi carp from marauding cats. To prevent the pool freezing over in winter, the carp are confined to the deep end of the pool, which is covered with sheets of bubble plastic, and then with loft insulation material. A small space is left uncovered, to let in oxygen.

Stepping stones are always watered before guests arrive, as Japanese gardens are traditionally supposed to look their freshest immediately after rain.

Grass lawns are not often found in Oriental gardens – moss is more commonly used. In time, the central grass area will be replaced with a moss sward. (Raked sand, fine gravel or pine needles or

beaten earth are other traditional alternatives.) Moss-like pearlwort (*Sagina glabra*) has already been tried, but looked too golden, so mosses will be used instead. They thrive and spread in light shade and moist soil.

Japanese ornaments

Statuary and stone ornaments are of less importance in Japanese gardens than in Western ones. Originally, they were purely functional or had religious significance; even today they are used with restraint.

Stone lanterns have been used for centuries, not for decoration, but to light a bend in a path, a bridge over a stream or the entrance to the tea house. Traditionally, a lantern is lit by candlelight and placed half-hidden by overhanging branches or with foliage plants shrouding its base.

Stone basins also belong to the ancient past. Carved from natural stone, they may be round or square, smooth or elaborately carved. They were placed close to the tea house so that guests could wash their hands before entering.

INDEX

feeding 70
'Félicité Perpétue' 43
'Golden Wings' 41
'Iceberg' 44
'New Dawn' 50
old-fashioned 158
'Orange Sensation' 90
prostrate 146
shrub 9, 100, 102, 158
standard 43, 145, 148
weeping 147
Rosemary 97, 99-100, 112-13, 115,
148, 164
Rudbeckia 96, 122
Rushes 149, 152

S

Sage, Bethlehem 48
Sagina glabra 'Aurea' 106, 172
Sagittaria 52
Sago palm 64
Salvia 31
Salix 123
Sandpit 10, 49-50, 99-100
Sanguinaria 93
Santolina 147-8
Sasa palmata 153
Saxifraga 123
   S. fortunei 107
   'Tumbling Waters' 107
   S. umbrosa 157, 159
Scree beds 6-7, 103, 105-8
Screens 15-16
Sculptures 4, 18-9, 59-60, 65, 67-8, 134
Seating area 24, 31, 34, 50, 52, 72, 74,
105, 107, 113, 162
Secluded gardens 55-60
Sedum acre 32
   S. spectabile 75
Sempervivum 32, 122, 156
Senecio 40-1, 44, 50, 101, 120, 141
   S. clivorum 52
   'Sunshine' 67
Sequoia sempervirens 'Adpressa' 32
Setts, granite 14, 47, 73-4, 76
Shade-loving plants 60, 69, 74, 103-4,
107
Shady gardens 15, 103-8
Shrubs 13, 17, 22, 28, 59, 81, 113, 144,
155
   border 45, 47, 125
   dwarf 32, 156
   evergreen 98
   ground-cover 82
   wind-resistant 136
Sink gardens 156
Sisyrinchium 118
Skimmia japonica 104, 107
Smoke tree 44, 96, 120
Snowdrop 34, 93, 126
Soil 13, 15
   acid 15, 93, 103, 114, 123
   chalky 15

improving 61-2, 67
light 15
loam 15
mulch 94
sandy 15
Solidago x hybrida 49
Solomon's seal 60
Sorbus 124, 153
Spartina pectinata 106
Speedwell 80
Spiraea japonica
   'Golden Dome' 41
   'Goldflame' 96
Spruce 32, 83, 93
Spurge 99, 101
Stachys 41, 101
Steps 46-7, 50, 71-4, 76
   brick 56-7, 63-4, 67, 98
   concrete 64
   shallow 66-7, 80
   York stone 67
Stipa gigantea 52
Stone, simulated 10, 17
Stonecrop 32
Stranvaesia davidiana 159
Suburban gardens 6-7, 91-6
Sumach 90, 140-1
Sweet Cicely 147
Sweet pea 31
Sweet William 30, 127, 147
Sweet woodruff 52, 54

T

Taxus baccata 55, 83, 93, 118
Theme gardens 135-72
Thrift 82, 148
Thuja occidentalis 32, 41, 93, 125
   T. orientalis 107, 124
   T. plicata 83
   topiary 164
Thujopsis dolobrata 32
Thyme 80, 86, 113, 115, 123, 148, 164
Tobacco plant 99, 102, 122, 126
Topiary 38, 63-4, 145, 161-6
Town gardens 3, 61-4, 117
Trachelospermum jasminoides 64
Trachycarpus fortunei 141
Tradescantia 68
Tree of heaven 86, 90
Tree peony 156
Trees 12, 13, 17, 22, 28, 66
   pollarding 61
   pruning 61
Trellis 21, 43, 55, 62, 65, 67, 98, 114
   trompe l'oeil 131-2, 134
Trillium 93
Trompe l'oeil 129-34
Trough gardens 156
Trumpet creeper 64
Tubs 38
Tulip 30, 54, 64, 66-7, 68, 69, 96, 102,
138, 158
   'China Pink' 51

'Clara Butt' 102
'Garden Party' 102
'General de Wet' 102
'West Point' 51
'White Triumphator' 51
Twinspur 160
Typha miniata 52

U

Urns 11, 14, 40, 44, 60, 105-6, 144-5

V

Vegetables 10, 15, 17, 24, 46-7, 49-50,
114
Verbascum 'Gainsborough' 41
Verbena 68
Veronica 32, 80
Viburnum 76, 82, 116
Vinca major 107
Vinca minor 98, 107-8
Vine, ornamental 44, 55, 63-4, 115
Viola cornuta 107
Violet 93, 147
Virginia creeper 38, 63-4
Vitis coignetiae 55, 57, 121
   V. vinifera 115, 141

W

Wake robin 93
Wallflower 30, 66, 68-9
Walls
   brick 15-16, 38, 52, 55, 57, 61, 65, 67,
79, 82, 97, 101, 104
   drystone 78
   low 34, 80-1
   plants 39-40
   retaining 16, 23, 51
   stone 73
Water feature 72, 74
Water iris 106
Water lilies 34, 106, 151
   miniature 52, 54
Weigela 91
Whitebeam 124
Wild strawberry 106
Willow 125-7
Wind barriers 85-8
Window-boxes 37-8, 40
Wisteria 3, 39, 44, 68, 127-8, 171

Y

Yew 81-4, 93-4, 103-4, 113, 116, 118, 121,
148
   hedge 49-50, 55
   topiary 161-2
Yucca 52, 54, 59, 141, 153-4

ACKNOWLEDGEMENTS

Photographer's credits
Peter Baistow 161-166; Eric Crichton 9(b),
10(t,c), 12, 21(t), 22, 43(b), 79-84, 131(t),
(designer Peter Aldington) 155-160, (designer
Graham Bell) 103-108, (designers Chris and
Freda Norton) 91-96; Eaglemoss/Eric
Crichton 45-50, 111-116, 123-128, (designer
Wendy Wright) 97-102; Eaglemoss/Andrew
Lawson (designers Mr and Mrs Kenneth
Watson) 167-172; ECC Quarries Ltd 10(b);
Garden Picture Library (John Glover) 78,
(Marijke Heuff) 143-149, (Ron Sutherland)
38(t), 61-63, 110, 149-154, (Brigitte Thomas)
2-3, (Steven Wooster) 130-131; John Glover
front cover, 36; Jerry Harpur (designer
Michael Blood) 55-60, (designer Geoff Kaye)
137-142, (designer Arthur Turner) 29-34; Neil
Holmes 9(t), 38(b), (designer Colin Wells-
Brown) 65-70; Insight Photo Library (Linda
Burgess) 131(b), (Michelle Garrett) 129;
Georges Leveque (designer Erwan Tynan) 85-
90; S and O Mathews 39(b), 42-43; Tania
Midgley 23, 42(b), 43(t), 133(b), 134; Monarch
Aluminium Ltd 11(t); John Neubauer 51-54,
64; Clive Nichols 4-5, 8, 11(b), 14; Hugh
Palmer 21(b), 28; Philippe Perdereau/Brigitte
Thomas 37, 40, (designer Lesne) 71-76; Photos
Horticultural 132; Harry Smith Collection
117-122, 133(t); Elizabeth Whiting and
Associates (Anne Kelley) 39(t), (Michael
Nicholson) 6, 136; Rita Wuethrian 13.

Illustrators
Lynn Chadwick 66, 81, 86-87, 104-105, 118-
119, 146-147, 156-157, 162-163; Russell
Gordon-Smith 25, 26; Dee McLean 27; Vivien
Monument 19, 24, 72-73, 98-99, 139; Lindy
Norton 20, 22, 23; Coral Mula 15-16; Liz
Pepperell 17-18, 47, 50, 56, 113, 127.

 Typesetting SX COMPOSING, ESSEX; Printing & Binding PRINTER INDUSTRIA, GRÁFICA S.A. BARCELONA
Separations COLOURSCAN OVERSEAS CO PTE LTD, SINGAPORE; Paper PERIGORD-CONDAT, FRANCE 53-015-1